Ancaster and Mount Hope Ontario in Colour Photos, Saving Our History One Photo at a Time

Photography
by Barbara Raué
2016

Series Name: Cruising Ontario

Book 66: Ancaster (including Lynden and Jerseyville) and Mount Hope

Cover photo: 117 Wilson Street West, Ancaster, Page 33

Series Name: Cruising Ontario
Saving Our History One Photo at a Time

Book 33: Southampton
Book 34: Jarvis
Book 35: Hagersville
Book 36: Caledonia
Book 37: Simcoe
Book 38: Cambridge Part 1 – Galt Book 1
Book 39: Cambridge Part 1 – Galt Book 2
Book 40: Cambridge Part 2 – Preston
Book 41: Cambridge Part 3 – Hespeler
Book 42: Kitchener Book 1
Book 43: Kitchener Book 2
Book 46: Shelburne
Book 47: Alton, Mono and Caledon
Book 48: London in Colour
Book 50: Orangeville Beginnings in Colour
Book 51: Orangeville on Broadway in Colour
Book 52: Orangeville Book 3 in Colour
Book 53: Dundas in Colour Book 1
Book 54: Dundas in Colour Book 2
Book 55: Dundas in Colour Book 3
Book 56: Stratford
Book 57: Hanover
Book 58: New Hamburg Book 1
Book 59: New Hamburg Book 2 and Haysville
Book 60: Waterdown in Colour
Book 61: Burlington in Colour
Book 62: Stoney Creek in Colour
Book 63: Seaforth
Book 64: Aberfoyle, Morriston and Rockton
Book 65: Eden Mills and Area
Book 66: Ancaster and Mount Hope in Colour

Series Name: Cruising Ontario
Saving Our History One Photo at a Time
in colour photos

Books Available in Alphabetical Order:
Aberfoyle, Acton, Alton, Amherstburg, Ancaster, Arthur, Aylmer, Ayr, Bloomingdale, Brantford, Burlington, Caledon, Caledonia, Cambridge, Clifford, Conestogo, Delhi, Dorchester to Aylmer, Drayton, Drumbo, Dundas, Eden Mills, Elmira, Elora, Essex, Fergus, Guelph, Hagersville, Hamilton, Hanover, Harriston, Hespeler, Jarvis, Jerseyville, Kingsville, Kitchener, Linwood, Listowel, London, Lucknow, Lynden, Mitchell, Mono, Mount Forest, Neustadt, New Hamburg, Niagara-on-the-Lake, Oakville, Orangeville, Orillia, Owen Sound, Palmerston, Peterborough, Port Elgin, Preston, Rockwood, Seaforth, Sheffield, Shelburne, Simcoe, Southampton, St. Jacobs, St. Thomas, Stoney Creek, Stratford, Tillsonburg, Waterdown, Waterford, Waterloo, Wellesley, Windsor, Wingham, Woodstock

Book 113: Waterford
Book 114-116: Waterloo
Book 117-119: Windsor
Book 120-121: Amherstburg
Book 122: Essex
Book 123-124: Kingsville
Book 125-127: Woodstock
Book 128: Thamesford
Book 129-132: St. Marys
Book 133-136: Sarnia

Other Books by Barbara Raue

Coins of Gold

Arrows, Indians and Love

The Life and Times of Barbara
Volume 1: Inventions That Have Enhanced My Life
Volume 2: Entertainment That I Have Enjoyed
Volume 3: East Coast Trips
Volume 4: Olympics Have Always Intrigued Me
Volume 5: Wonders of the World
Volume 6: Caribbean Cruises We Have Enjoyed
Volume 7: Animals
Volume 8: Storms and Other Major Disasters in My Lifetime
Volume 9: Wars, Terrorist Attacks and Major Disasters

The Cromwell Family Book

Laura Secord Discovered

Daddy Where Are You? - memoir

Montana Series
Book 1: Montana Dream
Book 2: Life on the Montana Frontier
Book 3: Montana to Boston and Back
Book 4: Montana Sons Go to War

Visit Barbara's website to view all of her books
http://barbararaue.ca

Ancaster

The Parliament of Great Britain's Constitutional Act of 1791 created the Upper and Lower Canadian provinces (colonies) from the division of the Province of Quebec (1763-1791) colony. At this time, Upper Canada was sparsely settled (unlike the more established Lower Canada) and its land had not been officially surveyed. The Lieutenant-Governor of Upper Canada, John Graves Simcoe, set out to survey this new province to establish settlements and military roads.

The earliest European settlers to arrive and clear land in the mid-18th century in what would eventually become Ancaster were made up of American farmers travelling north searching for arable land, French-speaking fur traders, and British immigrants. Also arriving into this area around 1787 with the incentive of inexpensive land grants were the United Empire Loyalists loyal to the British crown who were fleeing from the United States after the 1776 American War of Independence. Britain's promise of free land brought many people who did not exhibit the same loyalty to the crown as the Loyalists. This eventually led to a series of defections, accusations and treasonous acts during the War of 1812 that precipitated the largest mass hangings in Canadian history, the so-called Bloody Assizes whose trial took place in Ancaster in 1814.

When Upper Canada was invaded by the United States during the War of 1812 its occupants were primarily of American ancestry. After the war the province had a more British-centered influence. Britain expected its colonies to purchase all essential finished goods needed for day-to-day living from the mother country in exchange for raw materials such as fur and lumber. However, this 'arrangement' proved to be very inefficient and impractical in practice so waterwheels, mills and factories were soon built in favorable towns in Upper Canada that had abundant water power, fertile soil, and good transportation access such as Ancaster that could provide the new settlers with much self-sufficiency.

The early English settlers were independent having emigrated not to perpetuate a mold but to escape from it. They scattered far and wide. The Loyalists chose areas where there were good soil or waterwheel sites.

In an age before steam power, the wilderness that would become Ancaster had an early economic advantage due to the fact that it existed amidst a natural break in the Niagara Escarpment. Even its relatively minor water resources were valuable because they were easily accessible. Ancaster had access to two very important First Nations roads, the Iroquois Trail and the Mohawk Trail intersecting in the area that eventually became Ancaster Village. The Iroquois trail was the most important transportation route in Upper Canada as it meandered down the escarpment from the future Ancaster into what would eventually become Hamilton, Ontario towards present day Lewiston, New York, eventually linking up with similar trails in New York.

In the other direction the Iroquois trail led from present day Ancaster to what became the town of Brantford, Ontario where the trail branched off into the Detroit Path and the Long Point trail. By 1770, the eighty kilometers Mohawk Trail was the escarpment accompaniment of the lakeside Iroquois trail. The Mohawk Trail ran parallel to the Iroquois trail and originated and diverged from the Iroquois trail in present-day Queenston, Ontario until reconnecting to the Iroquois Trail in present-day Ancaster at what is now known as the intersection of Rousseau and Wilson Street. By 1785, the Iroquois Trail passing through present day Ancaster had been widened to accommodate horse and buggy traffic. Another influential road that intersected the Mohawk Trail very close to Ancaster Village was the Twenty Mile road that followed the Twenty Mile Creek up to present day Smithville, Ontario and beyond. Ancaster had fertile soil and abundant fresh water which encouraged pioneer settlers to clear the land and plant crops for subsistence agriculture.

A wooden grist mill and sawmill were constructed here in 1791-92 by millwright James Wilson with financial backing from Richard Beasley, an affluent fur trader and entrepreneur. These were the only mills west of Grimsby for many years. In order to attract workers to his mills, Wilson needed to provide the social amenities and commercial framework for an area of land which was an isolated frontier forest with accessible water power situated at the juncture of well-established transportation trails. In that period the area was populated with just a smattering of First Nations aboriginal peoples and wilderness farmers. With Beasley's financial assistance, Wilson constructed a general store, a blacksmith shop, a distillery and a tavern within walking distance of his mills. Wilson's newly arrived employees began to build their homes in close proximity to their place of work. Wilson's primary residence was also used as a school, a magistrate's court and a cooperage.

By 1793 the area was surveyed and officially came to be known as Ancaster Township as chosen by John Graves Simcoe who was inspired in the name choice by Peregrine Bertie, the 3rd Duke of Ancaster and Kesteven, an ancient village and former Roman town that still exists in the district of Lincolnshire, England.

Wilson sold his interest in the mills and some adjoining land in 1794 to Jean Baptiste Rouseaux, Montreal born fur trader, interpreter, businessman, and militia officer who already had a home and general store on Wilson Street. Rousseaux's Ancaster general store traded with Joseph Brant's Mohawks and other Iroquois people from the Six Nations confederacy located at the Grand River. Rousseaux had been Governor Simcoe's official native and French interpreter and was a close confidante and advisor to native leader Joseph Brant.

After the War of 1812, the Egleston brothers built a farm equipment foundry; Job Lodor built a woolen mill; Eyre Thuresson built a threshing machine factory (now converted to a home); and Jasper Crane built an impressive stone four-storey knitting mill (1854-1875).

Rousseaux built the Union Hotel in 1797 on Wilson Street, which is now remembered as the location of the Bloody Assize trials in 1814 during the War of 1812. By building his hotel on Wilson Street, Rousseaux reversed the then trend of building exclusively on the Mohawk trail. Rousseaux also added a brewery and distillery and hired Ancaster's first school teacher. He was the first assessor, tax collector, magistrate and the Township's first Lieutenant Colonel of Militia. Rousseaux became a considerable land owner and assisted significantly with native relations, was able to bridge French and English cultures successfully and was instrumental in the early development of Ancaster and old York.

In 1871 the existing and currently well-maintained Ancaster Township Hall opened at a cost of $2,400. Additional examples of Victorian architecture are also located on Wilson Street, amongst them the Richardson residence, which was built in 1872 as a wedding present for Dr. Henry Richardson and his new bride Sarah Egleston. Other similar structures includes St. John's Church 1869, the Gurnett home 1826, Gurnett General Store 1826, Hammill house 1860, the Egleston house, Job Lodor's home 1820, Rousseau Hotel 1832 and the Thuresson home 1872. The oldest building in Ancaster is the Tisdale house at 314 Wilson Street, which was built c. 1806 and whose current function is a police museum.

The Brantford and Hamilton Electric Railway intersected Ancaster Village in 1907 making fresh milk and other perishable foods, general supplies and mail easily deliverable on a daily basis for the first time. The Ancaster Fair has been an annual agricultural and social event since 1850. The Town of Ancaster encompasses an area of sixty-seven square miles and includes the former communities of Lynden, Jerseyville, Carluke and Alberton.

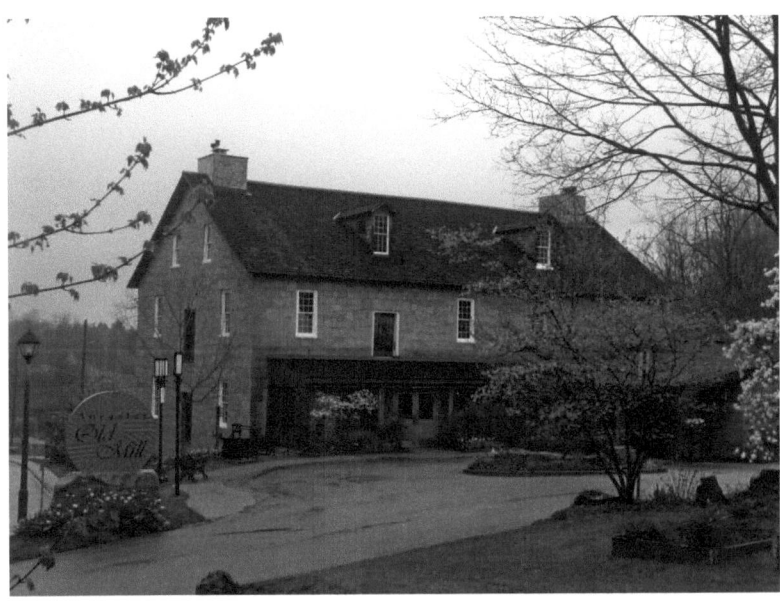

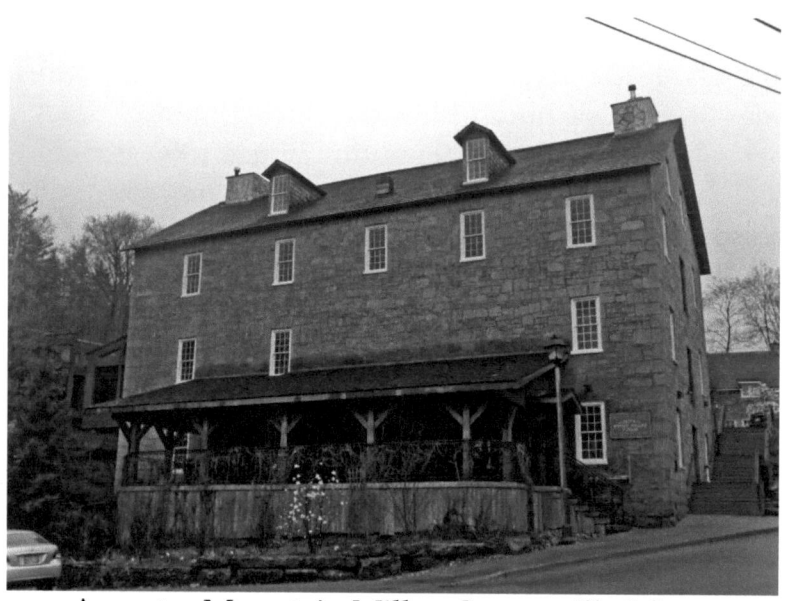

Ancaster Mountain Mills – Stone milled flour

The Ancaster Mill is one of the few remaining operating grist mills in Ontario. The original mill built south of Wilson Street in 1791 was destroyed by fire at the onset of the War of 1812 and replaced 300 yards downstream. The second mill burned and was replaced in 1818 on the present site. In 1854 this mill burned and was replaced by the present structure in 1863. The building is constructed of solid limestone walls with decorative corner quoins. The gable roof has two gabled-dormers on each side and the double-hung windows have flared stone lintels.

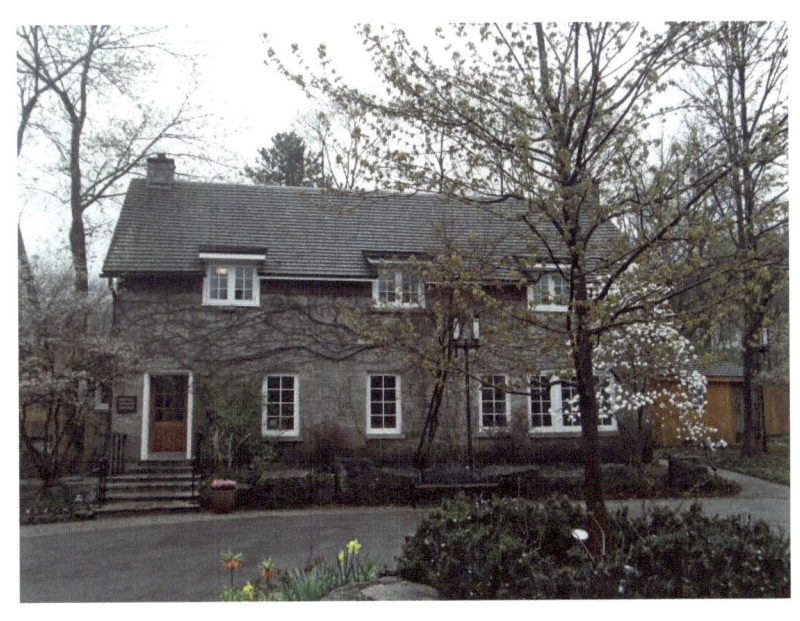

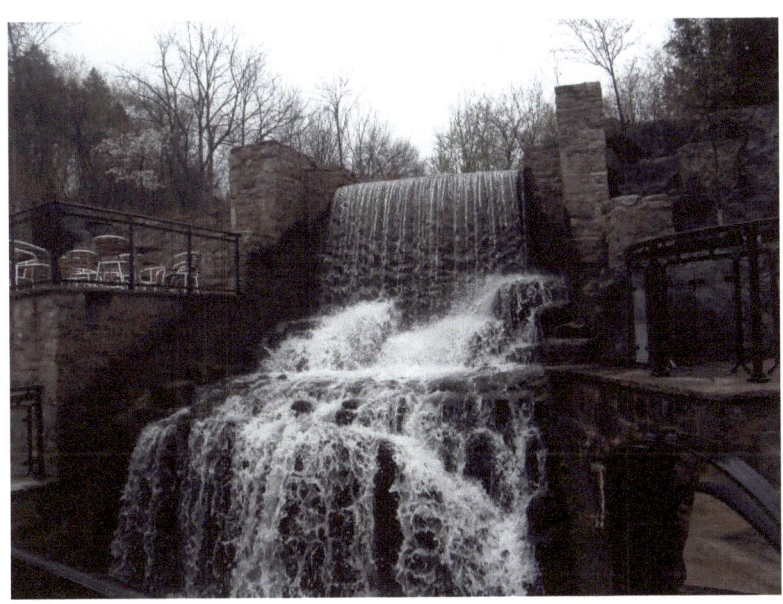

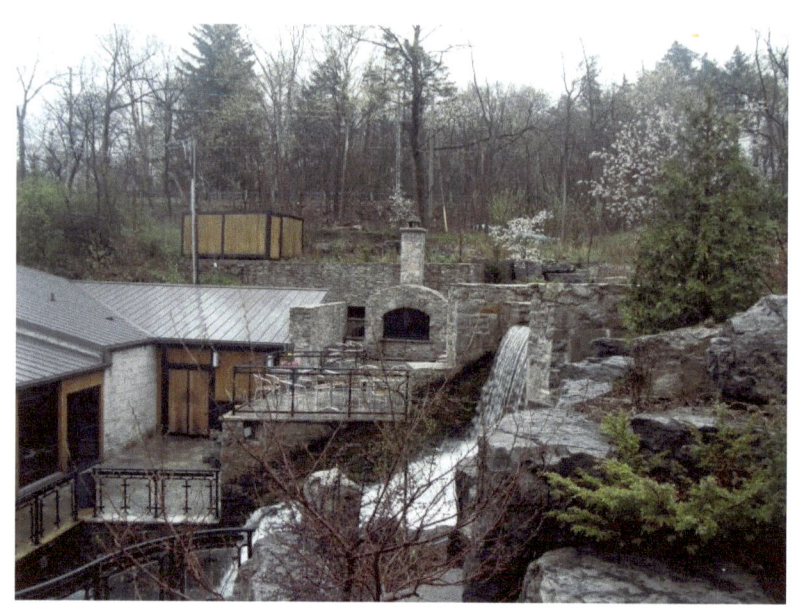

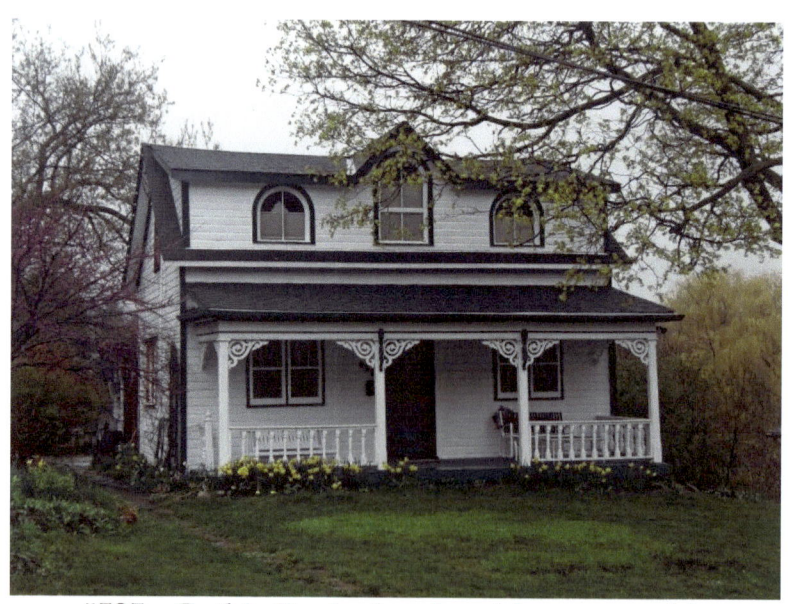

#535 - Gothic Revival style with centre gable

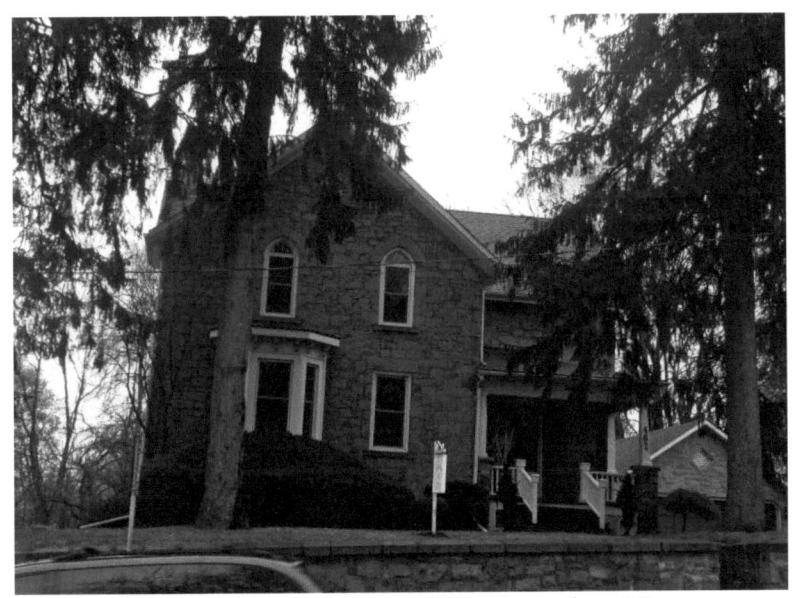

462 Wilson Street East - The Brandon House

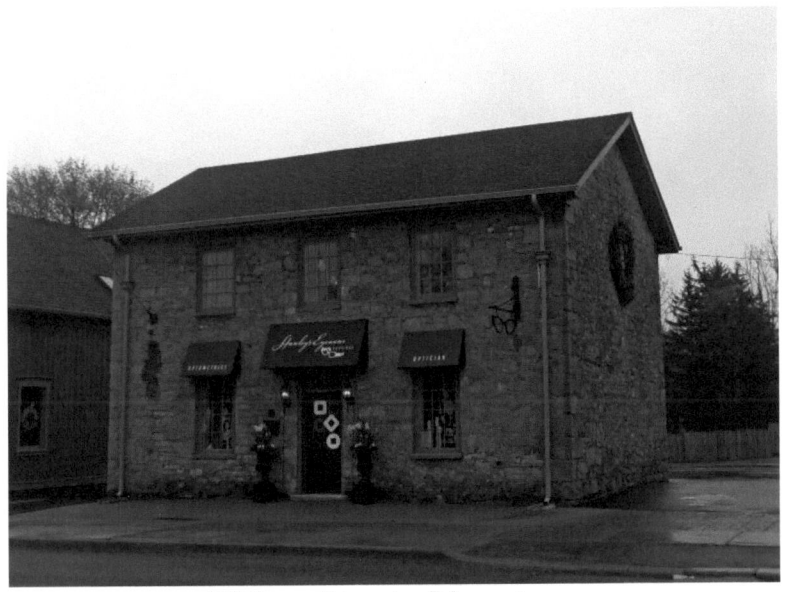

Wilson Street - Limestone

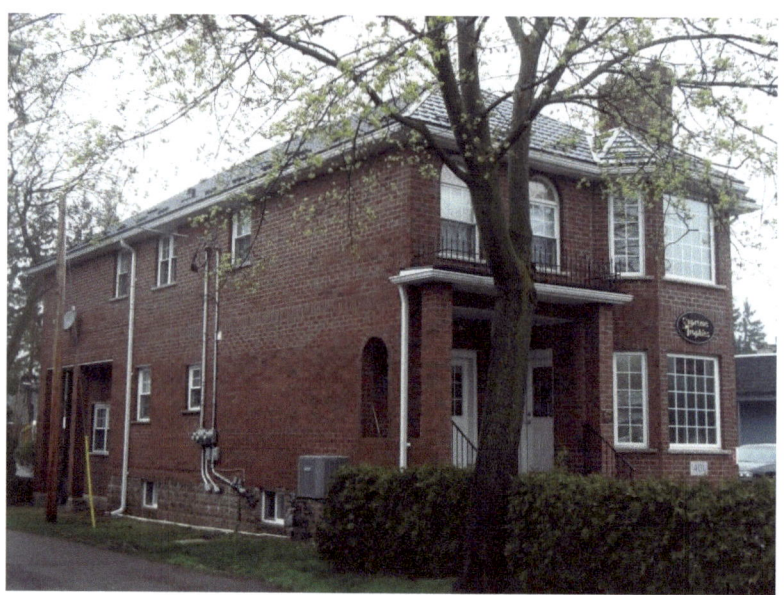

401 Wilson Street East – red brick

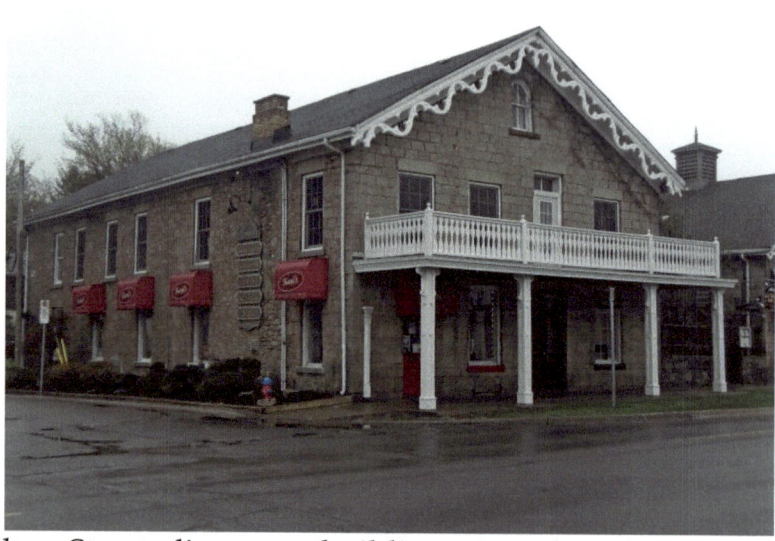

Wilson Street - limestone building, gingerbread trim, second floor verandah

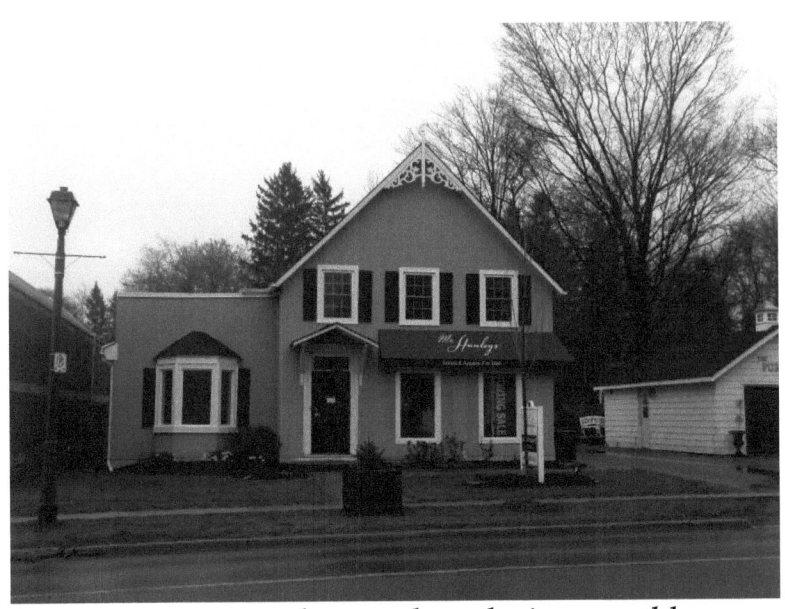

Gothic Revival, verge board trim on gable

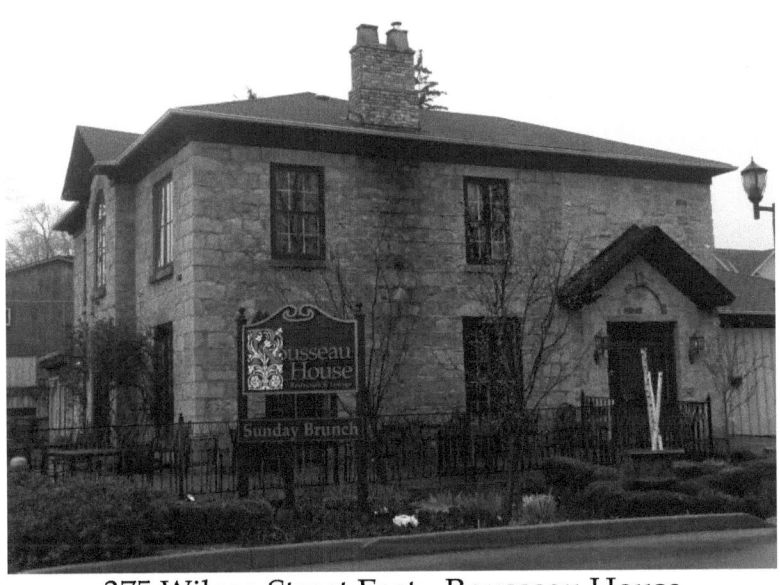

375 Wilson Street East - Rousseau House
- built in 1838 by George Brock Rousseau, postmaster of
Ancaster for ten years

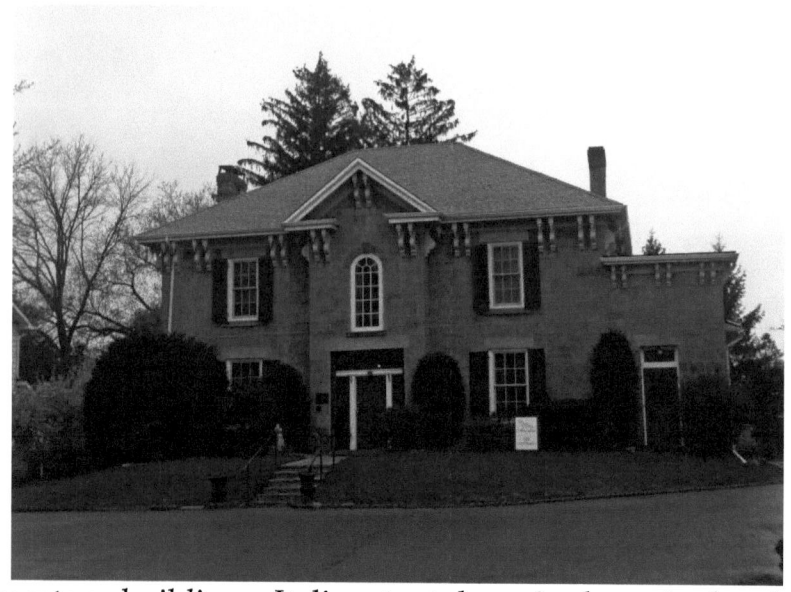

Limestone building – Italianate style, paired cornice brackets under the eaves, frontispiece, hipped roof, cornice return on gable

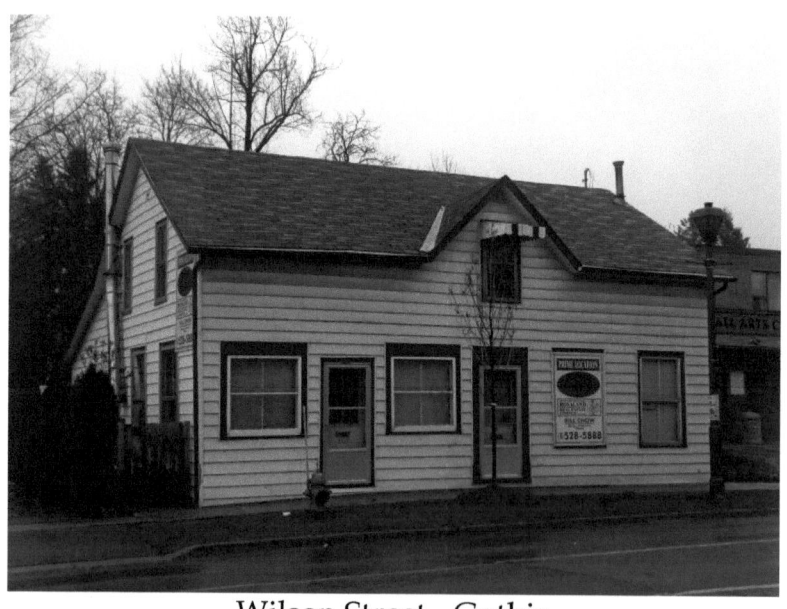

Wilson Street - Gothic

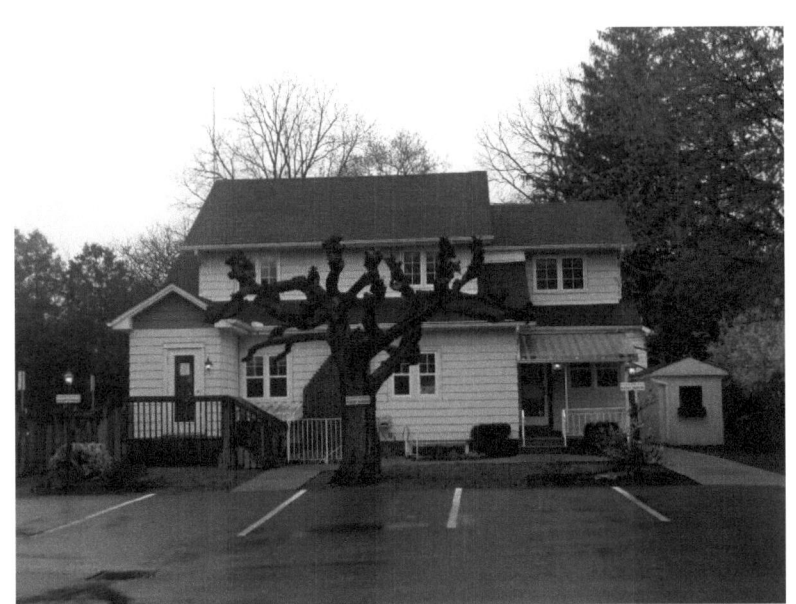

Wilson Street

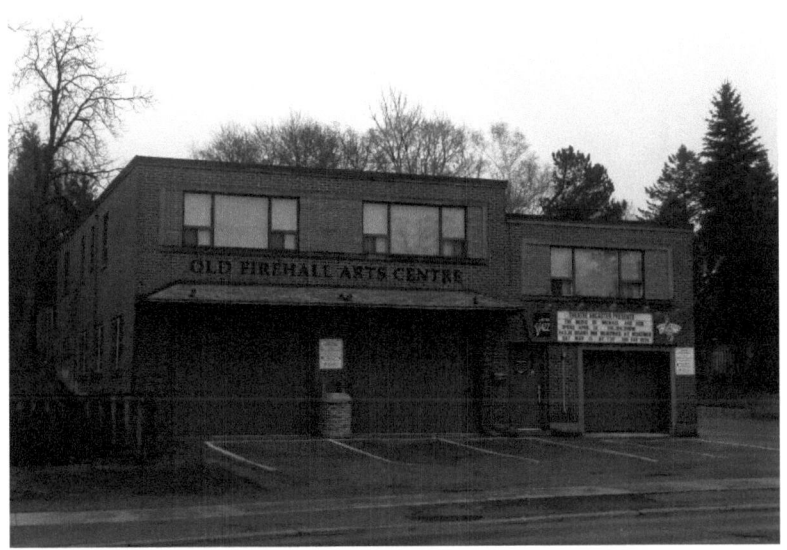

Wilson Street - old Fire Hall

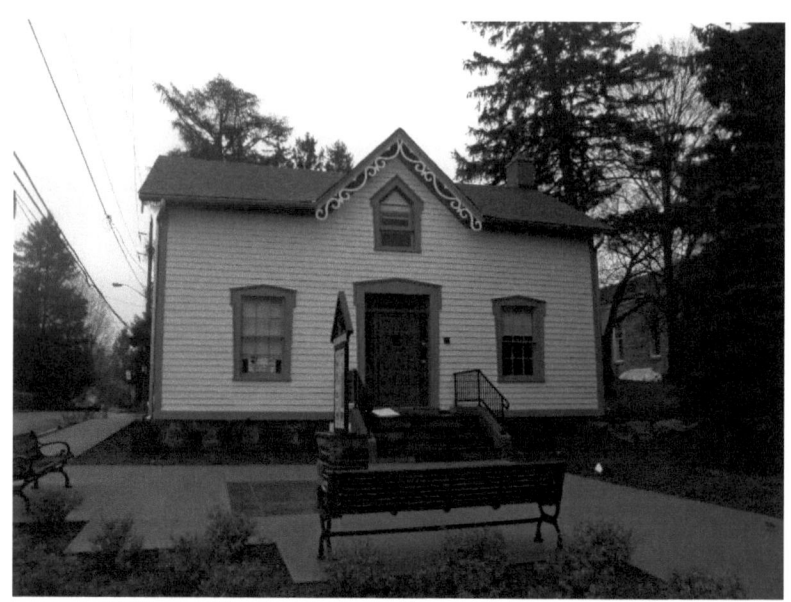

Wilson Street - verge board trim on gable

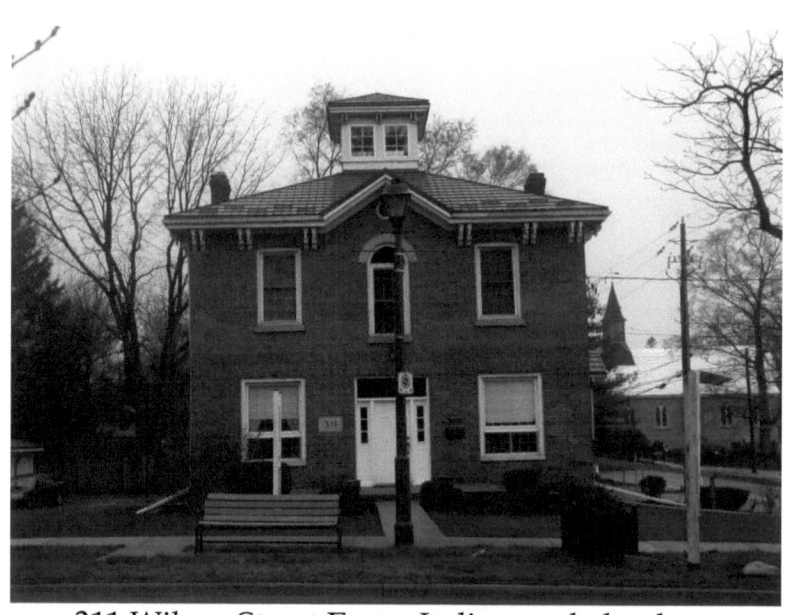

311 Wilson Street East – Italianate, belvedere,
paired cornice brackets

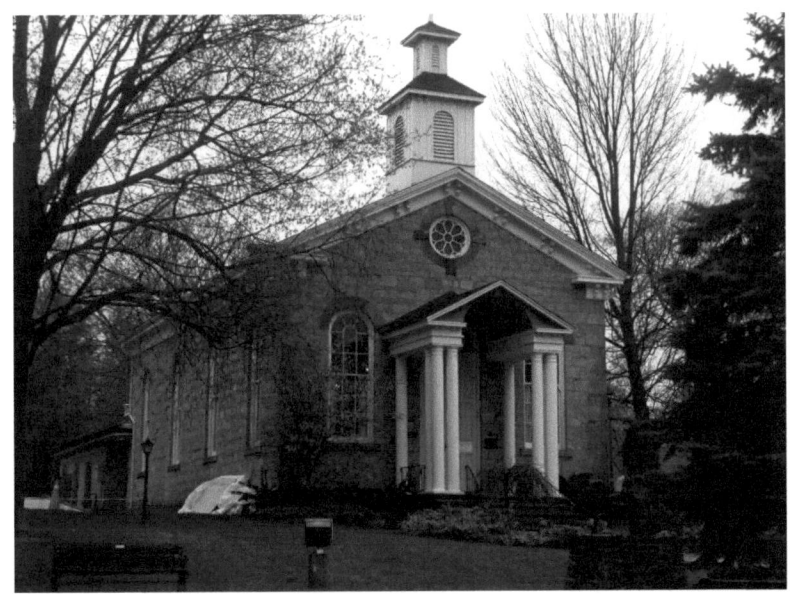

Wilson Street - Township Hall - constructed in 1871, a stone building in the Georgian style of architecture with a neo-classical portico and an Italianate cupola.

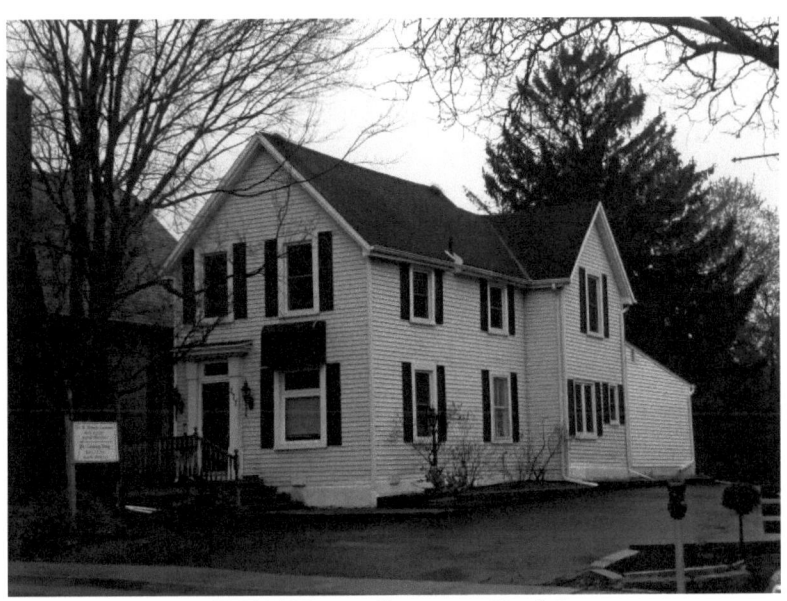

277 Wilson Street - Gothic

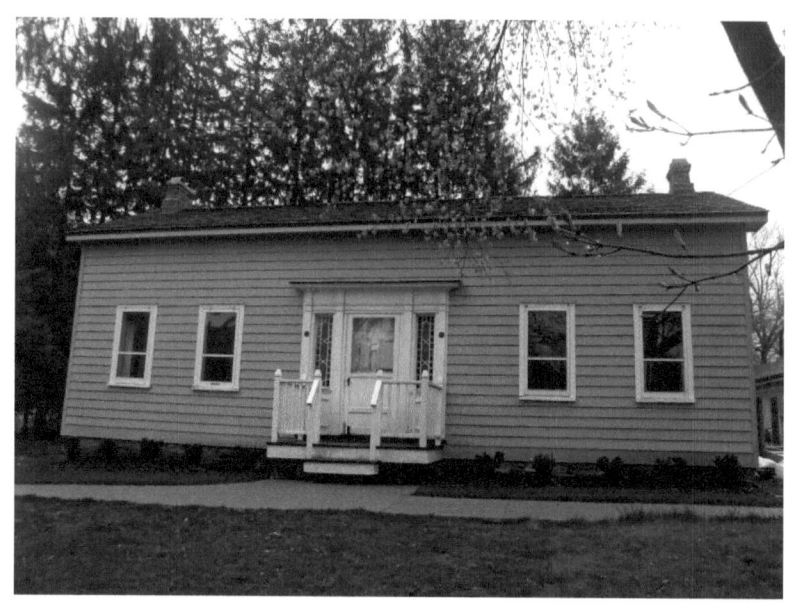

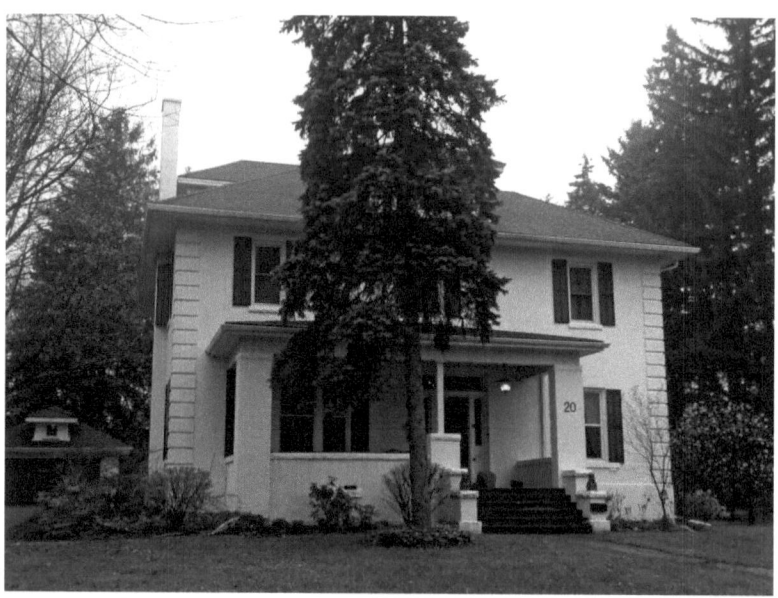

#20 - Italianate - hipped roof, corner quoins

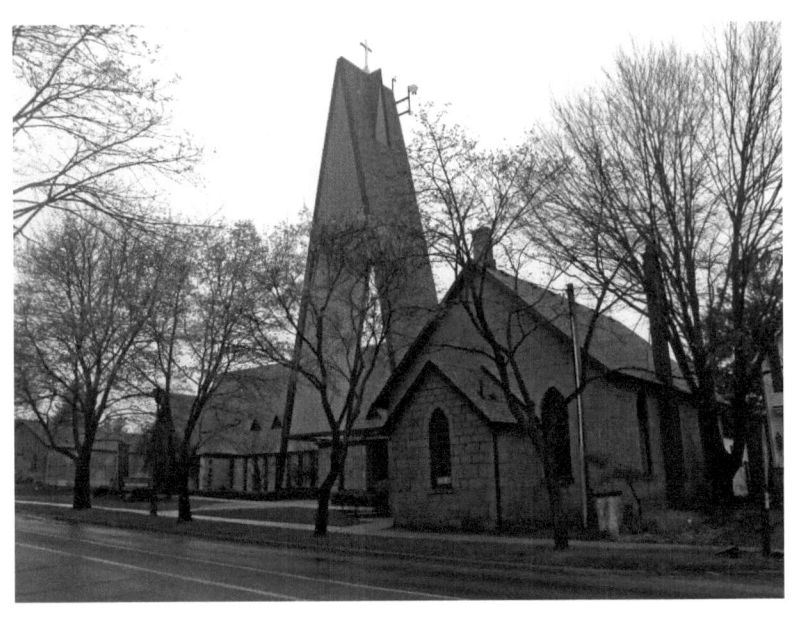

265 Wilson Street - Ryerson United Church

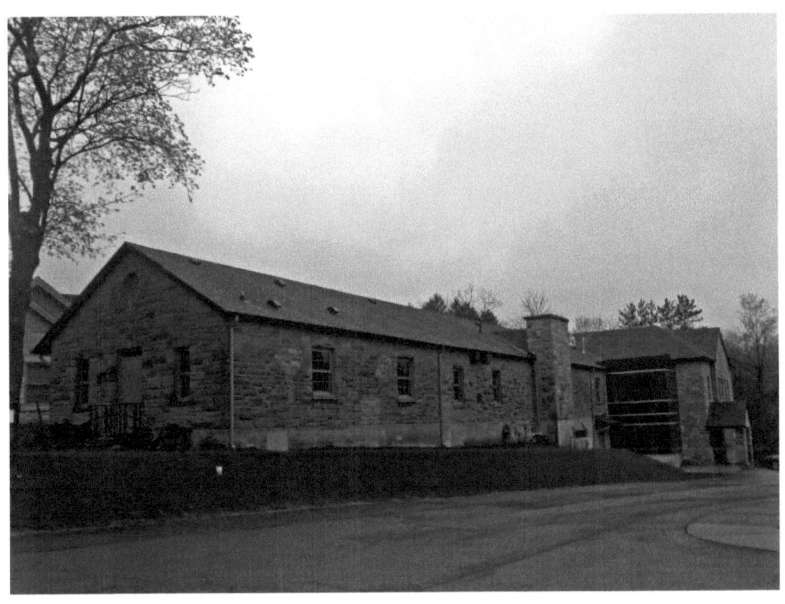

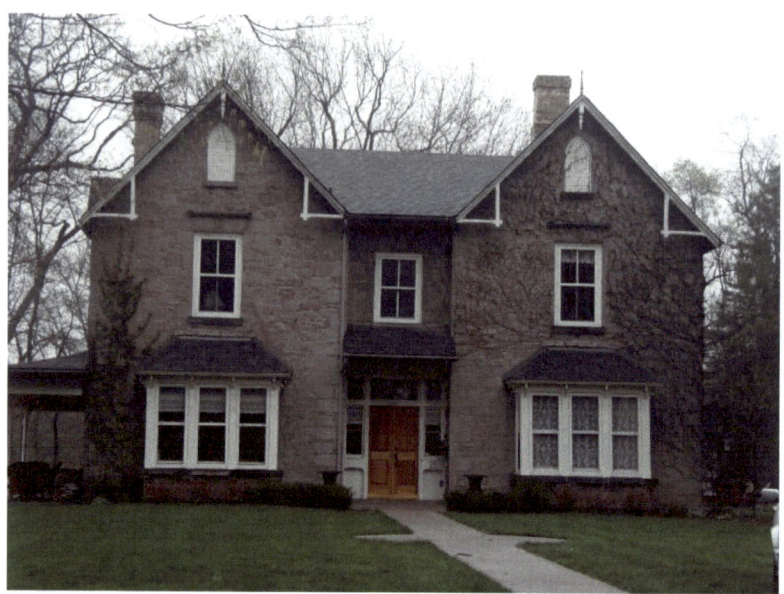

#21 – limestone building – Gothic Revival, sidelights, transom window, bay windows

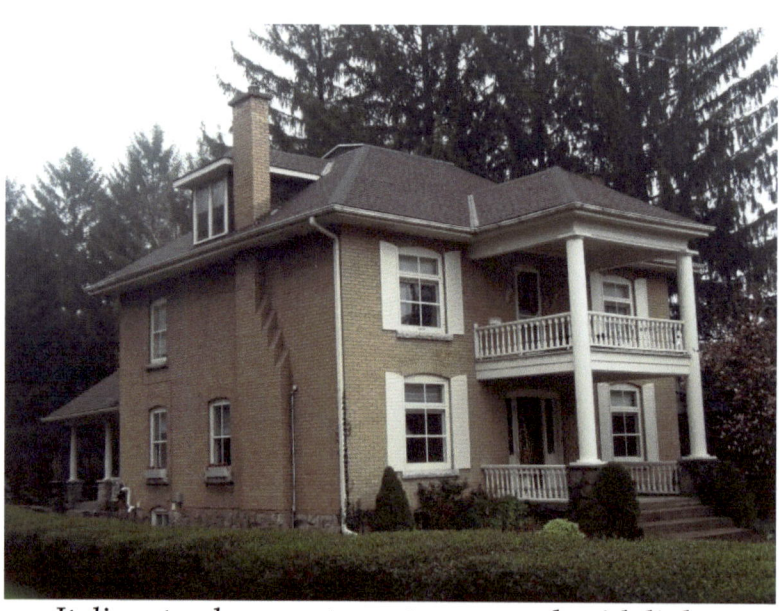

Italianate, dormer, two-storey porch, sidelights

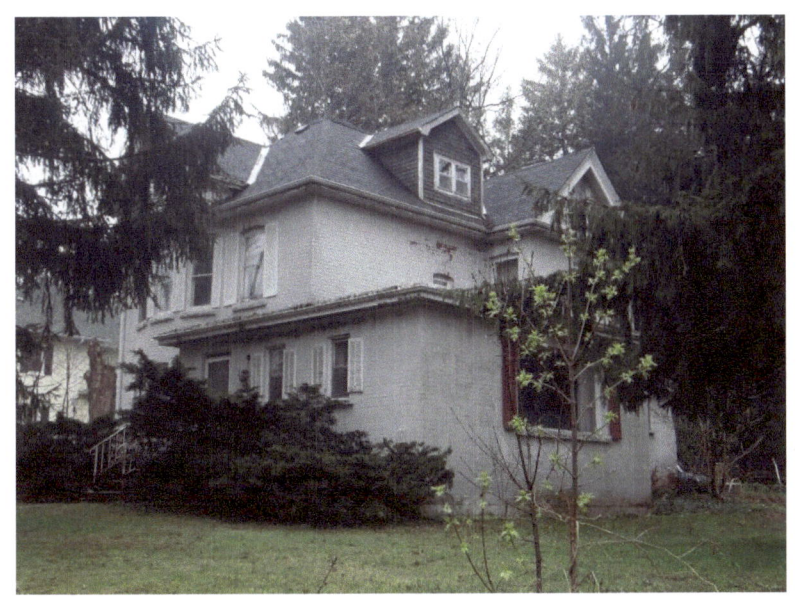

dormers

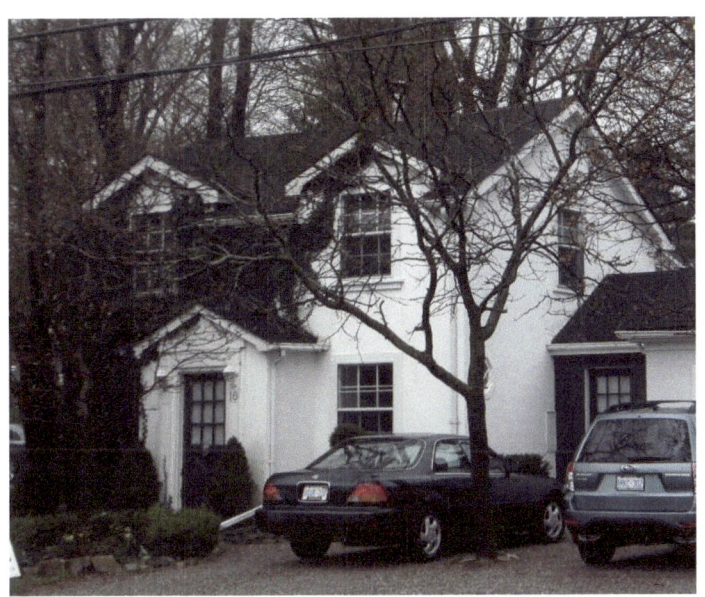

#16

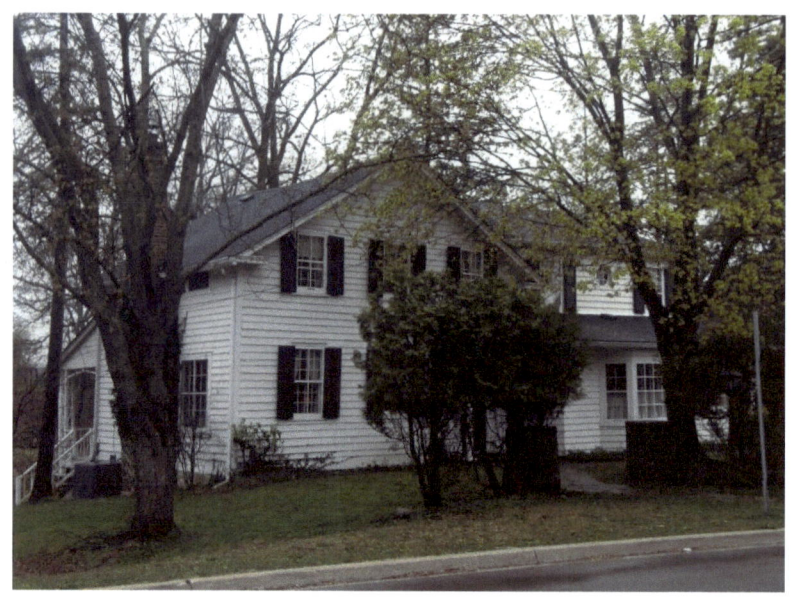

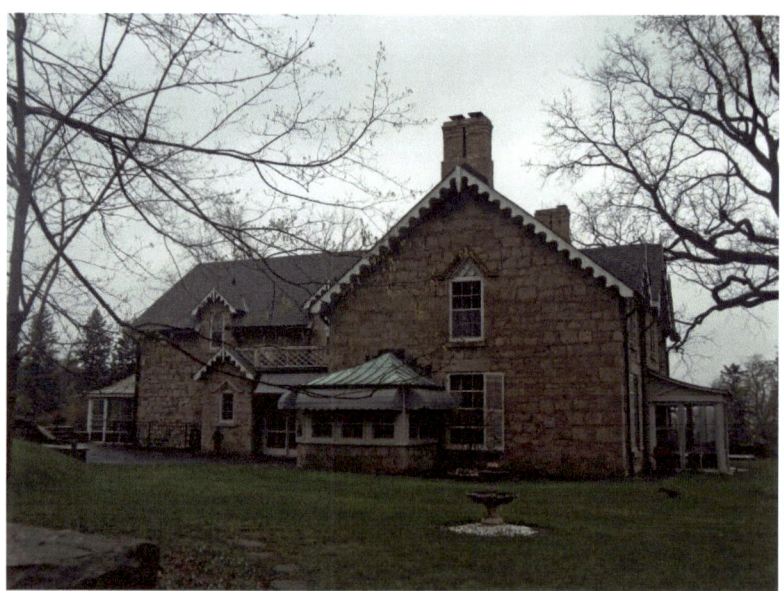

Fairview – verge board trim on gables

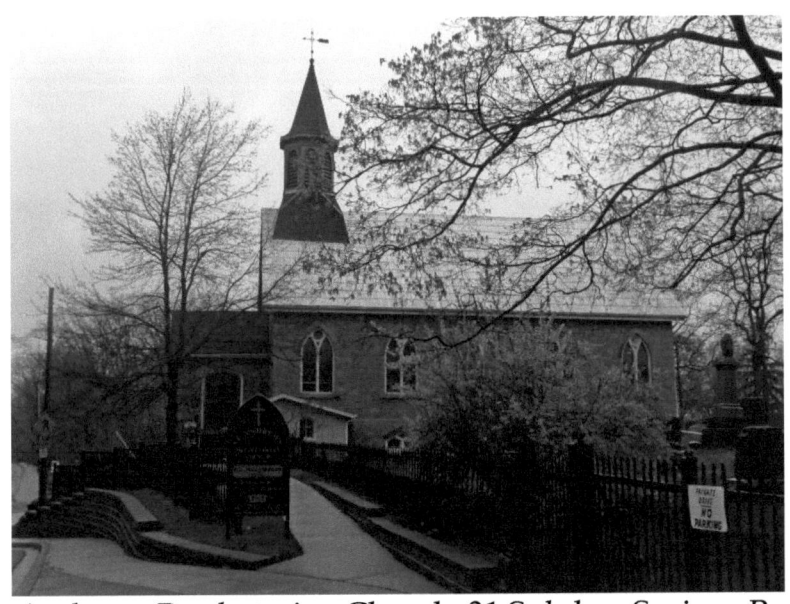

St. Andrews Presbyterian Church, 31 Sulphur Springs Road
Founded in 1826 – present stone building completed in 1875
Gothic, lancet windows

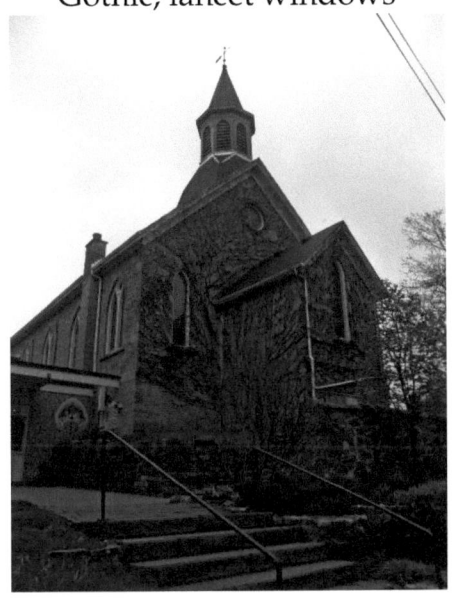

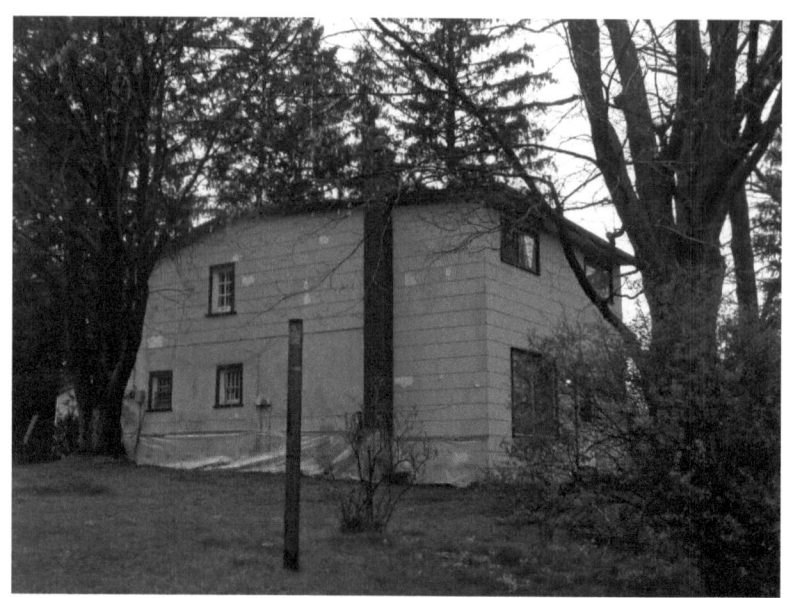

Jerseyville Road – rented for about 35 years
by Klaus and Judy Brandt

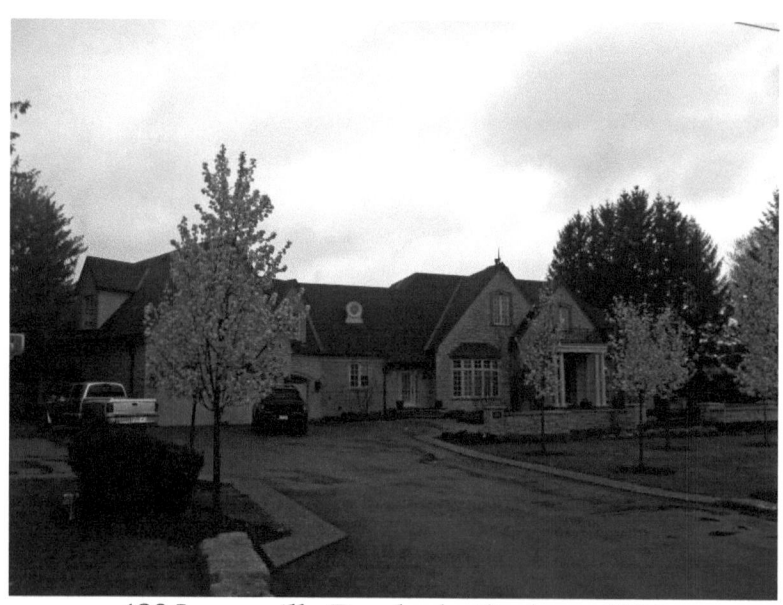

489 Jerseyville Road – built about 2008

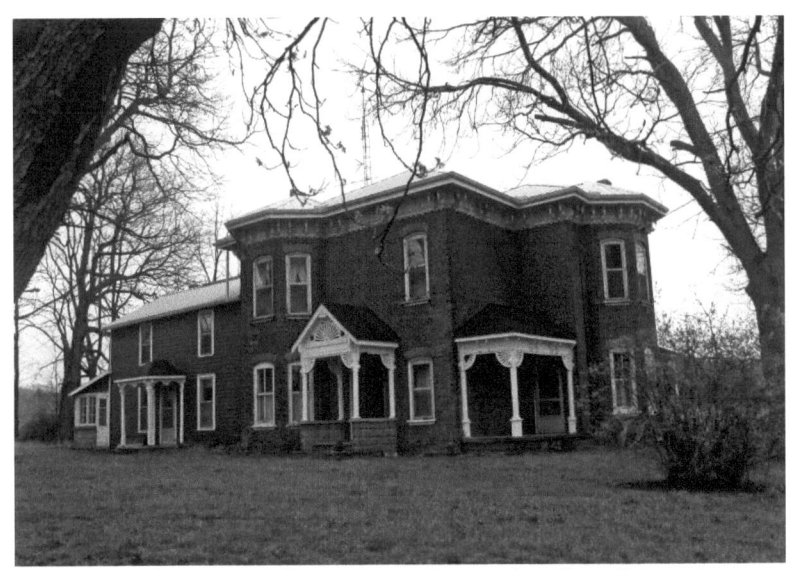

Italianate, hipped roof, cornice brackets,
bric-a-brac on porches

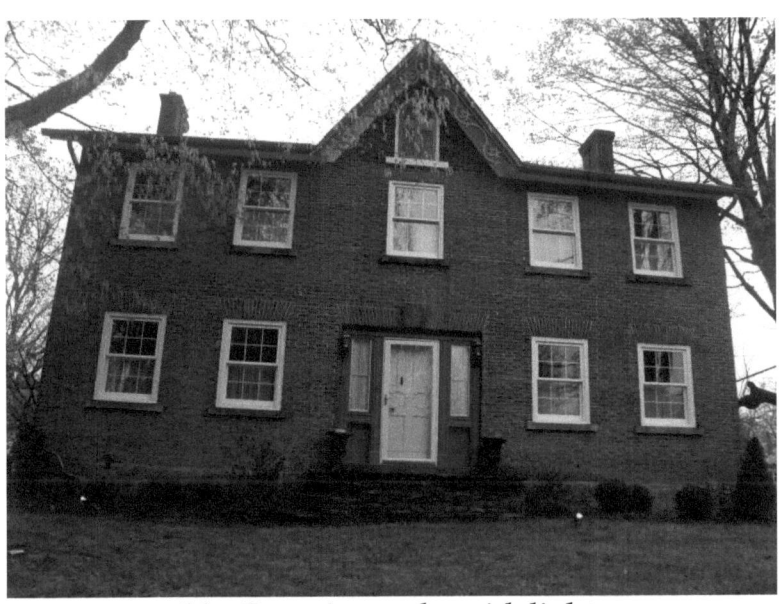

#6 - Georgian style - sidelights

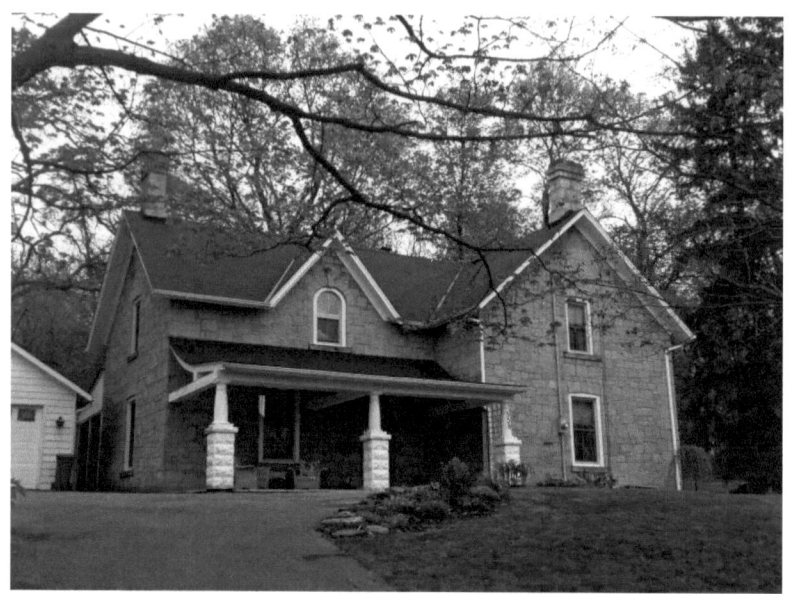

#558 – Gothic - limestone

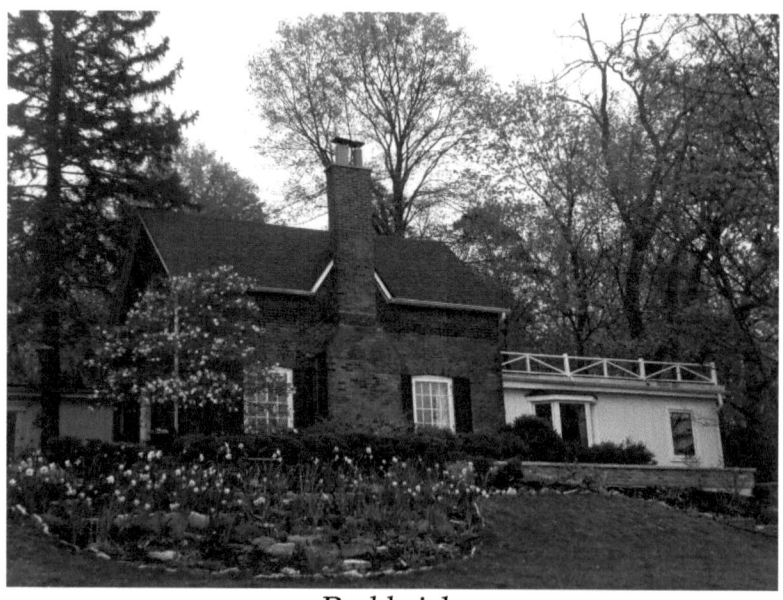

Red brick

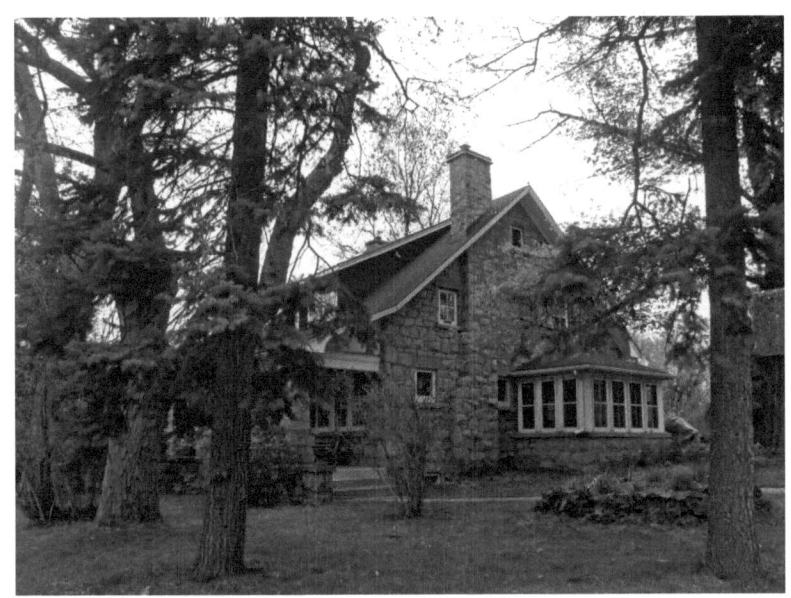

Cobblestone, bay window

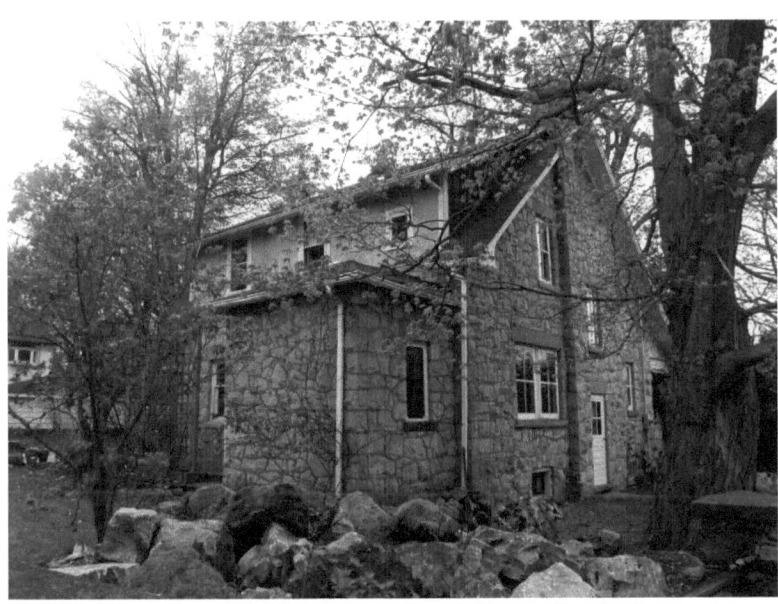

Rousseau - Cobblestone building, shed dormer

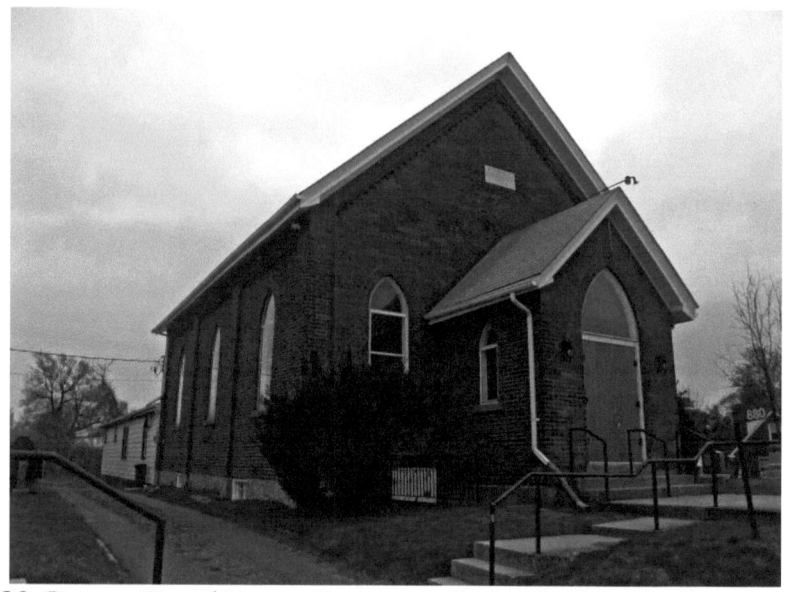

880 Garner Road East - Bowman United Church (formerly
Methodist – circa 1796) - joined the United Church in 1925
Gothic, lancet windows

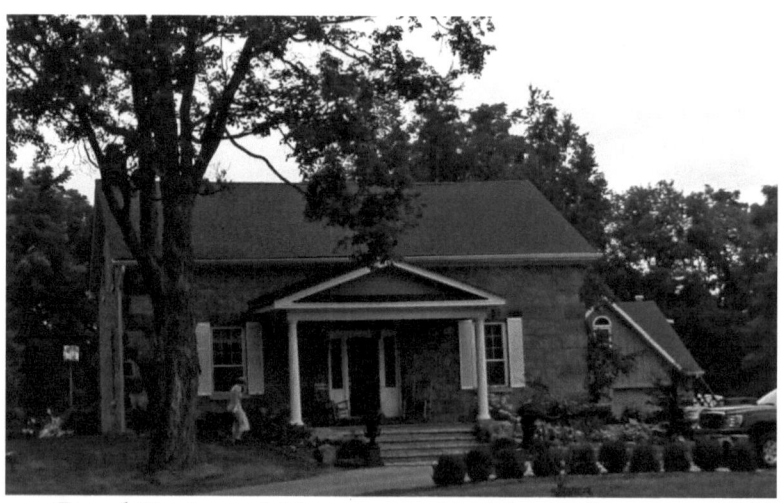

Garner Road East – cobblestone – Gothic, pediment, sidelights

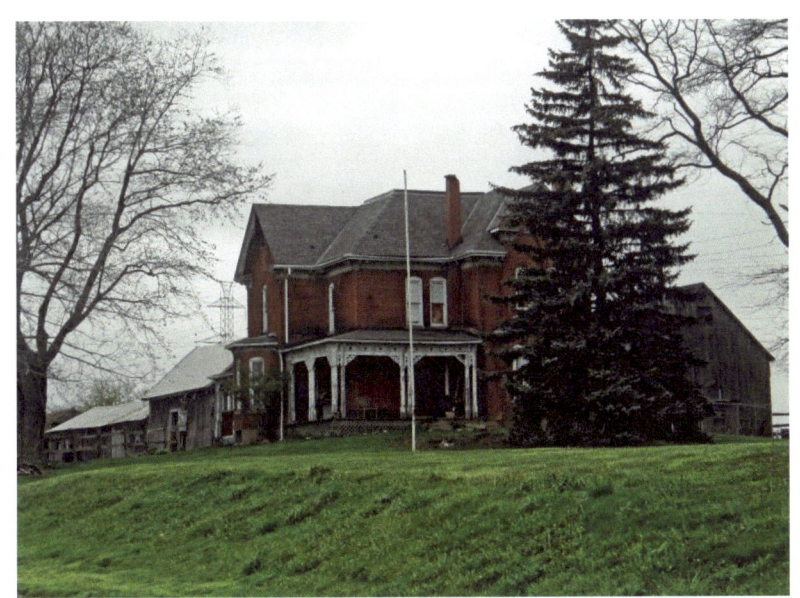
Bric-a-brac on verandah

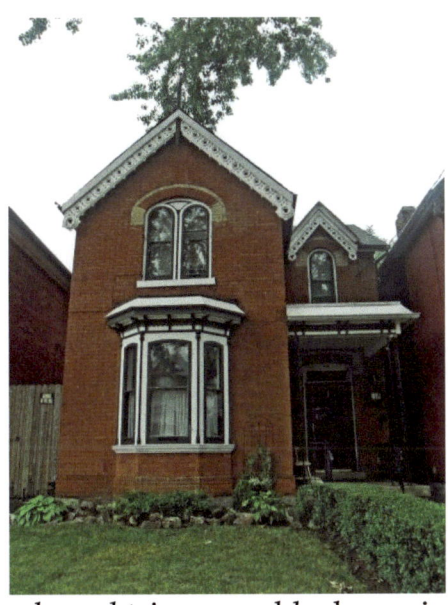
Verge board trim on gable, bay window

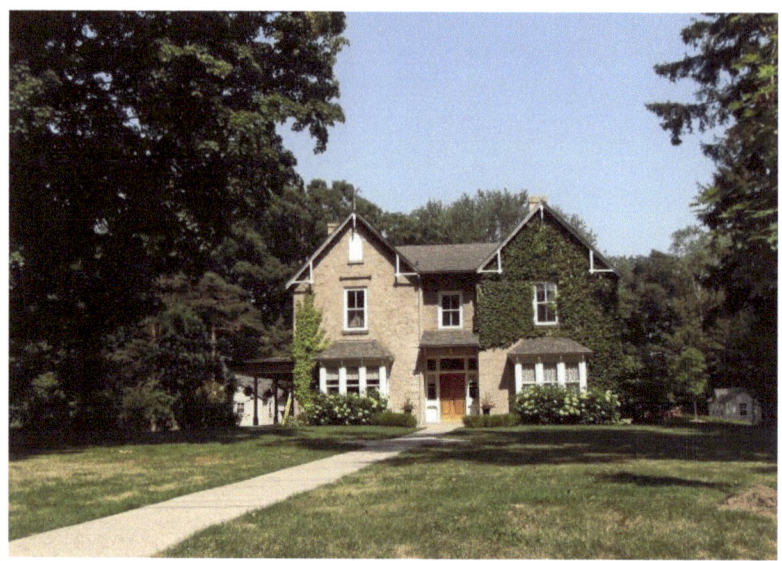

Halson Street – Gothic Revival – finial on gables, bay windows

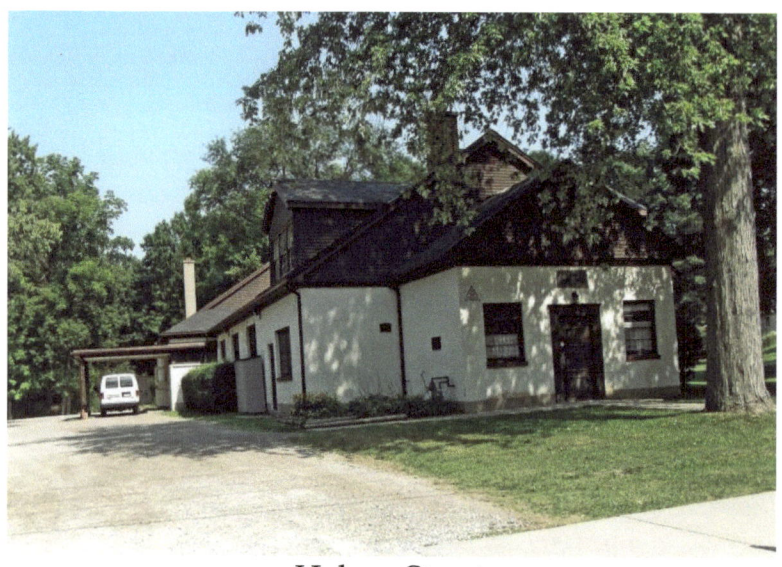

Halson Street

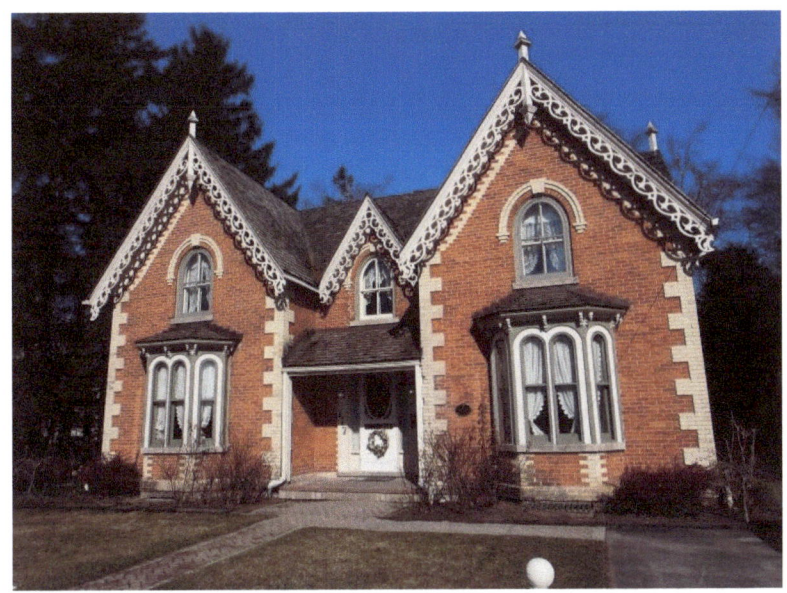

117 Wilson Street West – c. 1855 - Gothic Revival, two-storey red brick house, verge board trim and finials on gables, corner quoins, bay windows

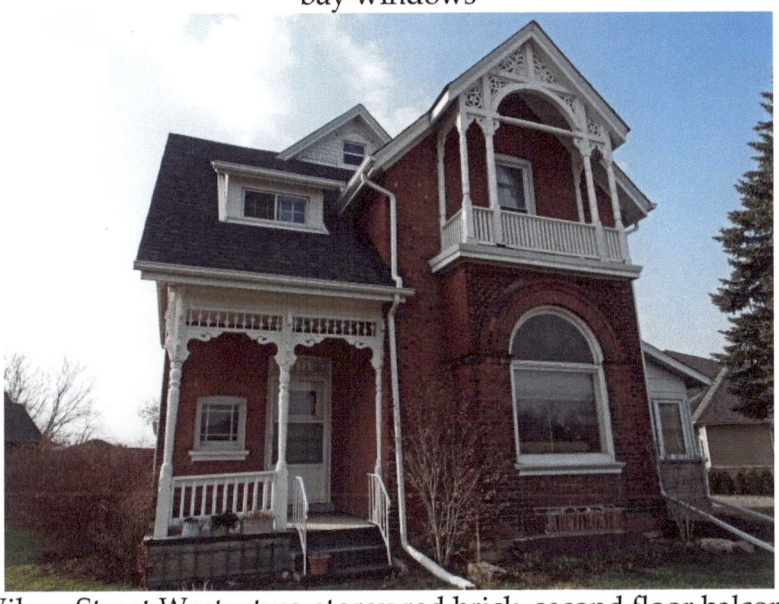

Wilson Street West – two-storey red brick, second floor balcony under gable which has stenciling on the verge board trim, dormer, bric-a-brac on lower porch

Jerseyville

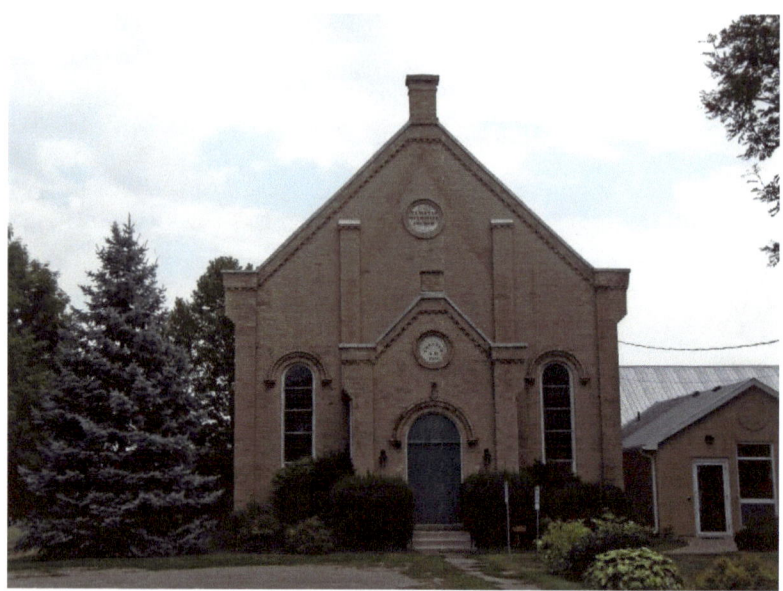

Wesleyan Methodist Church erected A.D. 1860

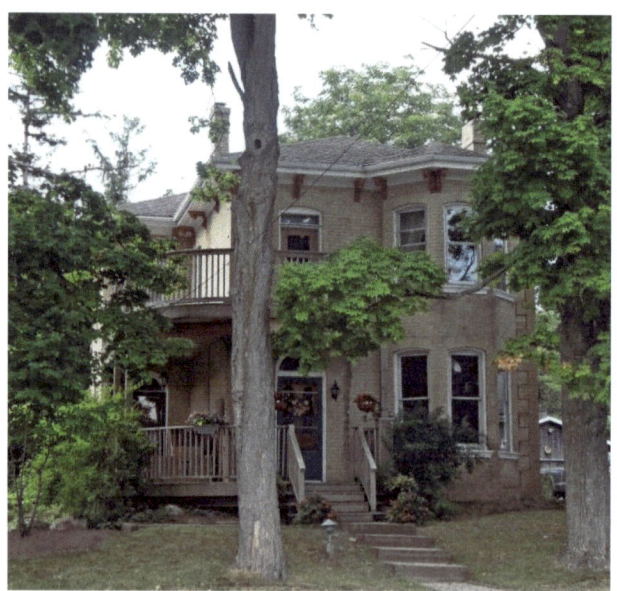

Italianate style – hipped roof, cornice brackets

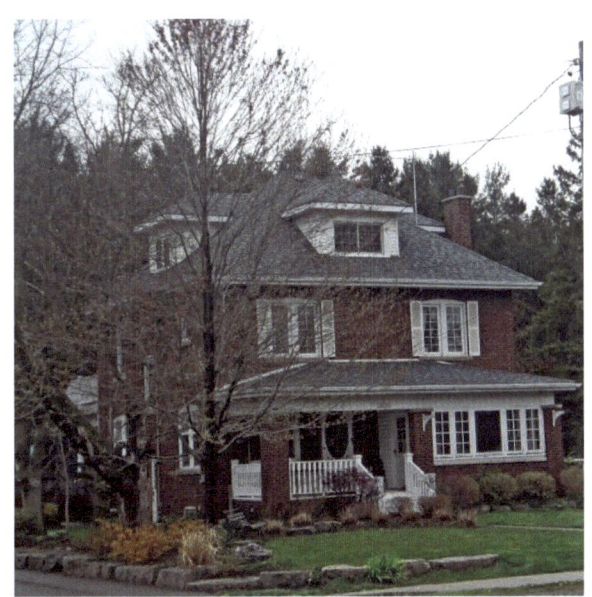

Italianate – hipped roof with dormers

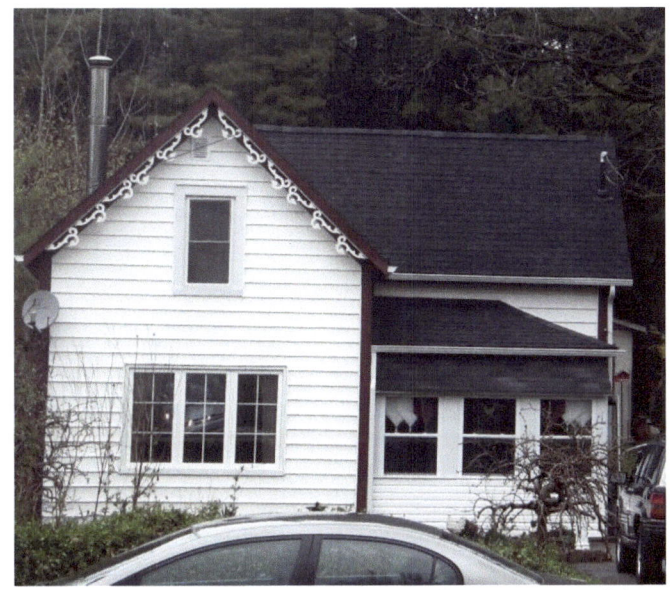

Gothic Revival – verge board trim on gable

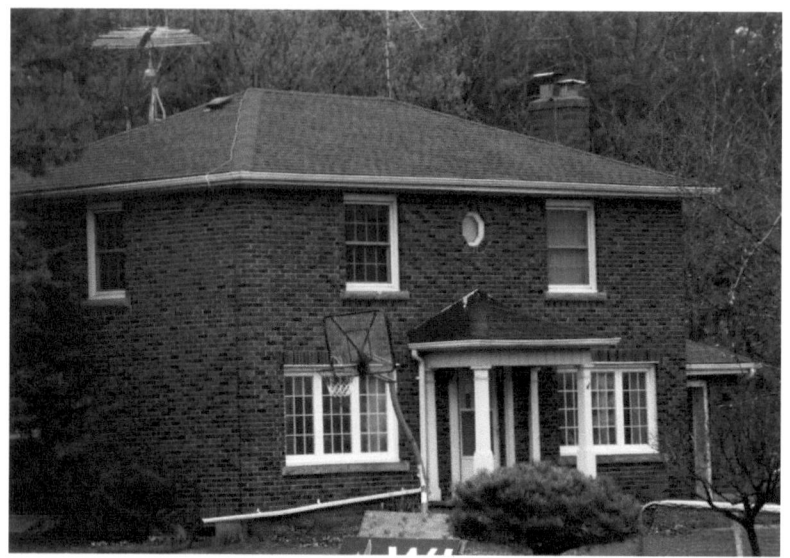

Italianate – hipped roof

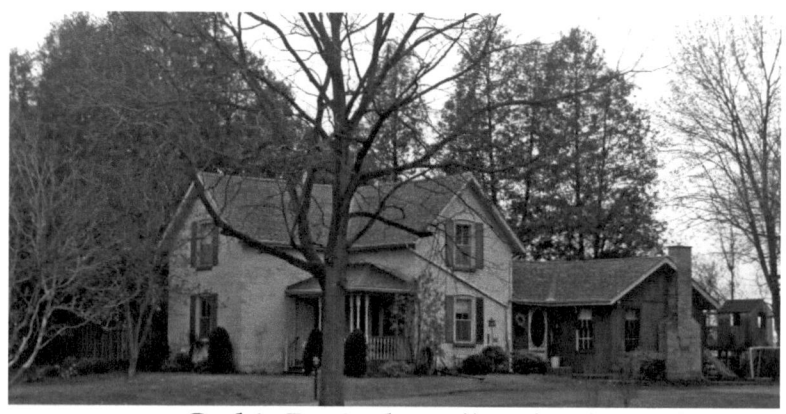

Gothic Revival – yellow brick

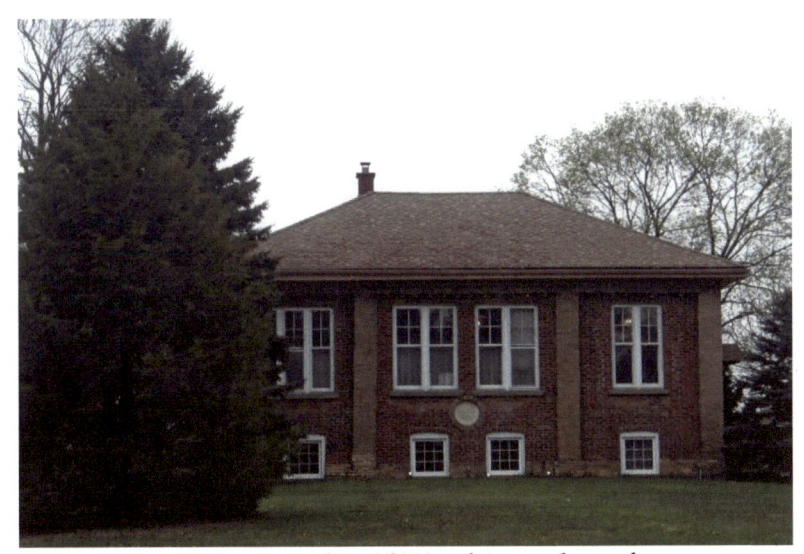

S. S. No. 10 – 1874 – hipped roof

Lynden

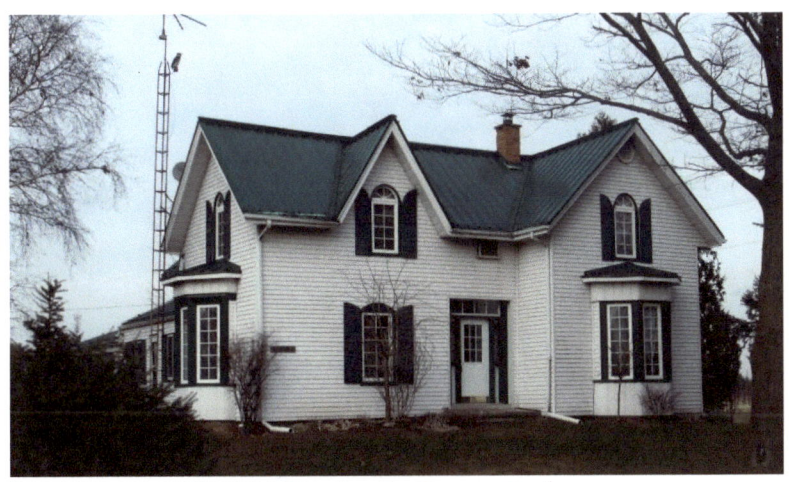

Gothic Revival - bay windows

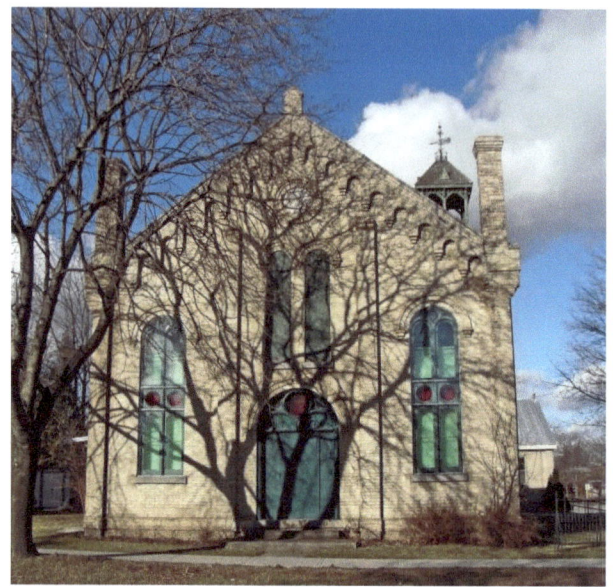

Governor's Road – Lynden United Church

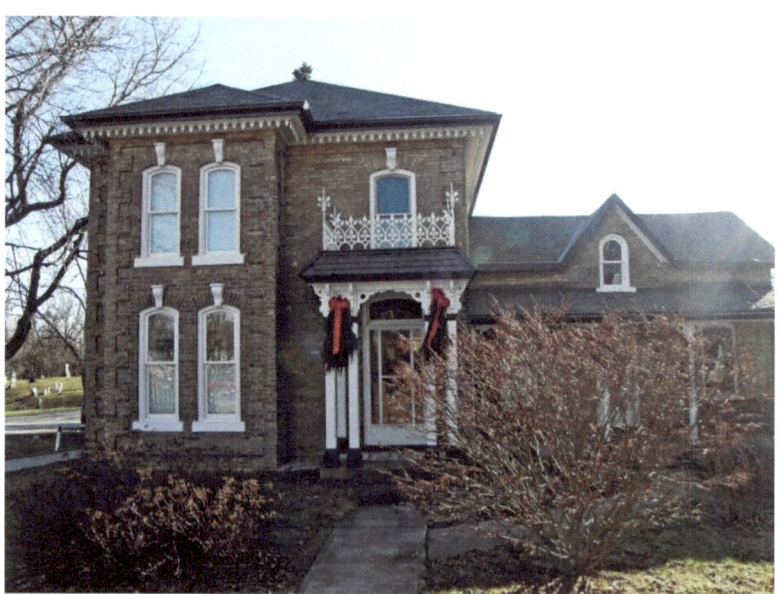

Italianate – hipped roof, decorative cornice, voussoirs and keystones, iron cresting above entrance, corner quoins

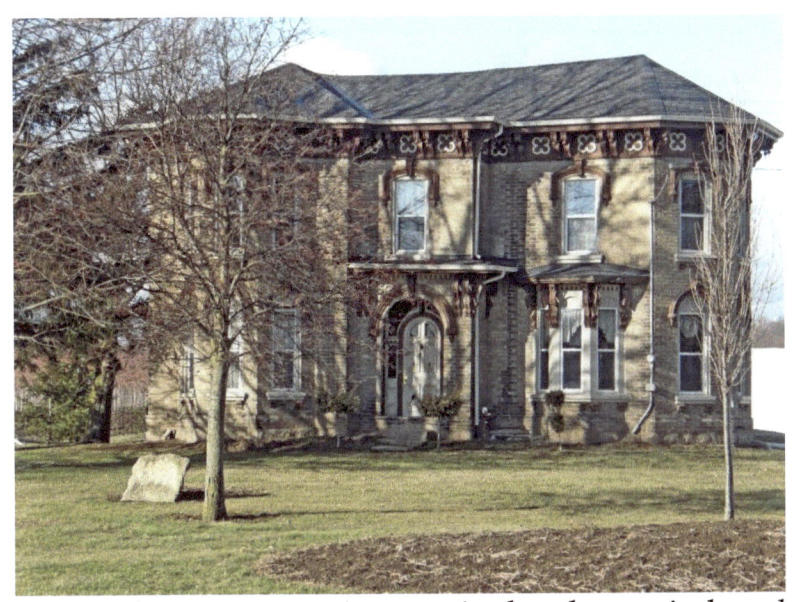

Italianate, decorative cornice, cornice brackets, window drip molds with keystones, bay windows

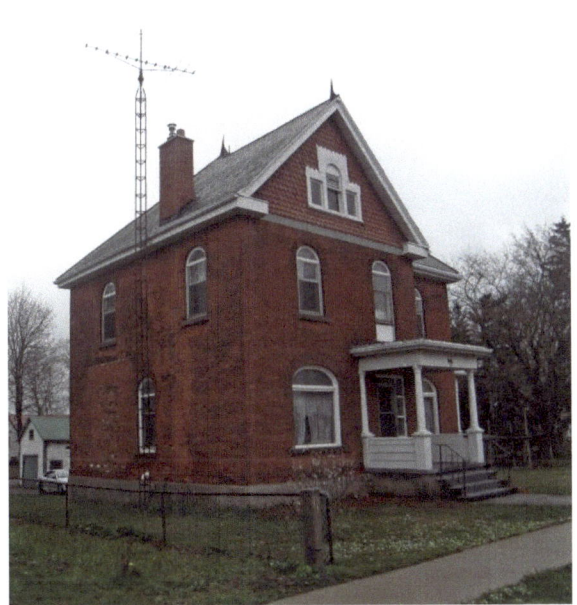

Edwardian – Palladian window

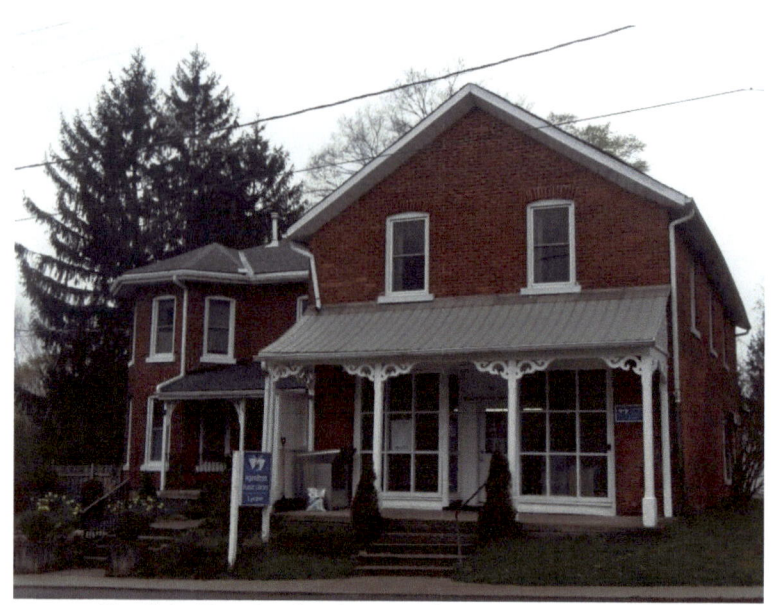

Gothic Revival – bric-a-brac on verandah

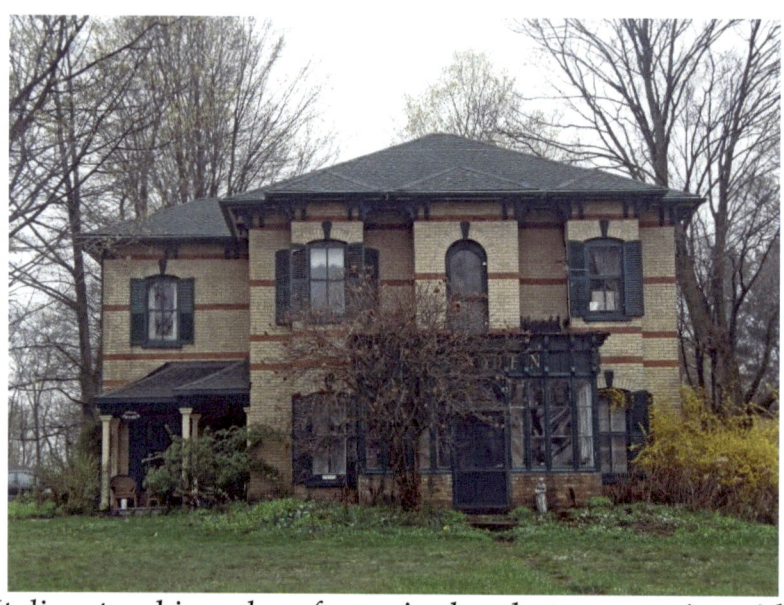

Italianate – hipped roof, cornice brackets, voussoirs with keystones, banding

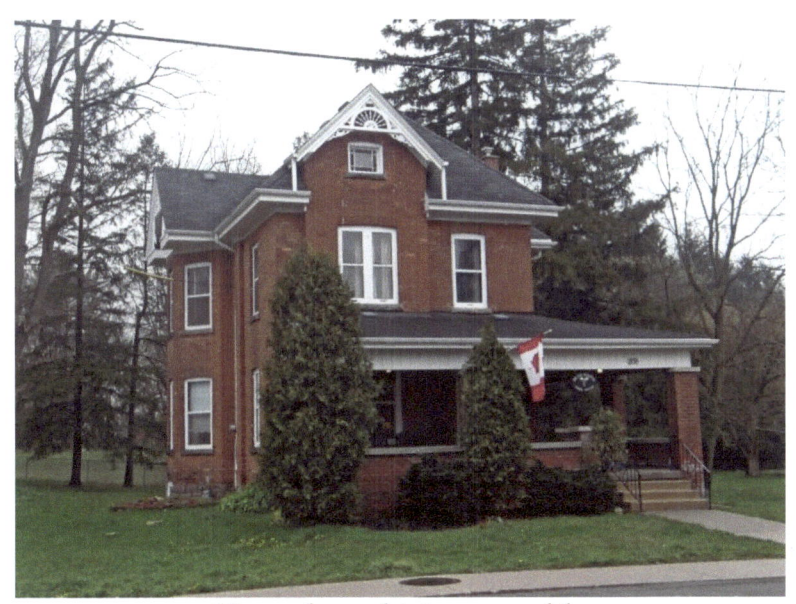

Verge board trim on gable

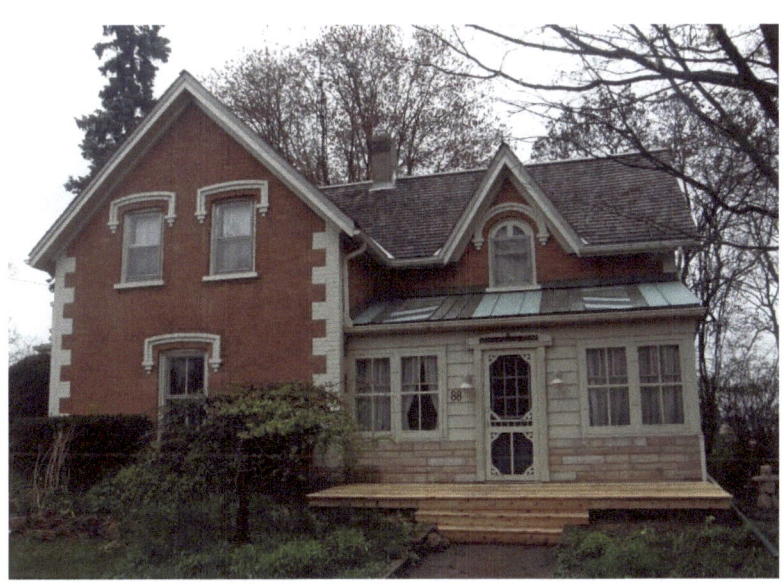

Gothic Revival – corner quoins

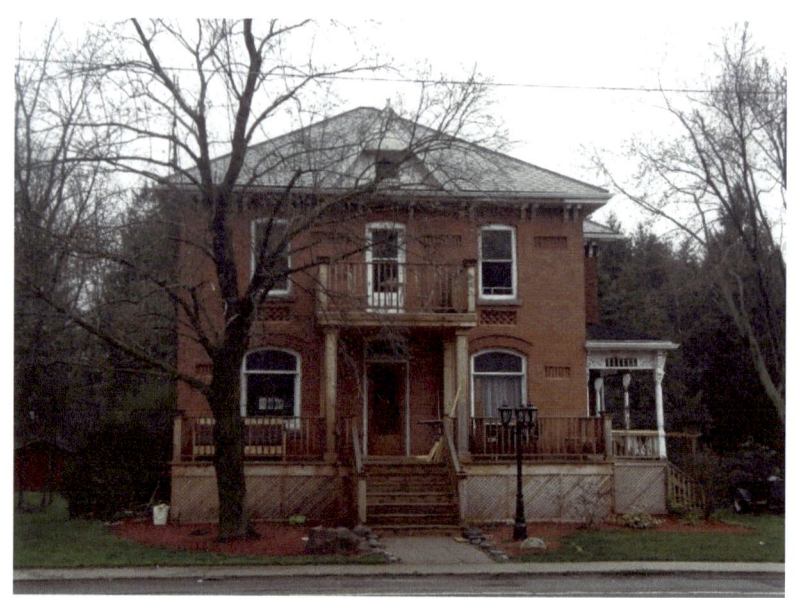

Italianate – hipped roof, second floor balcony

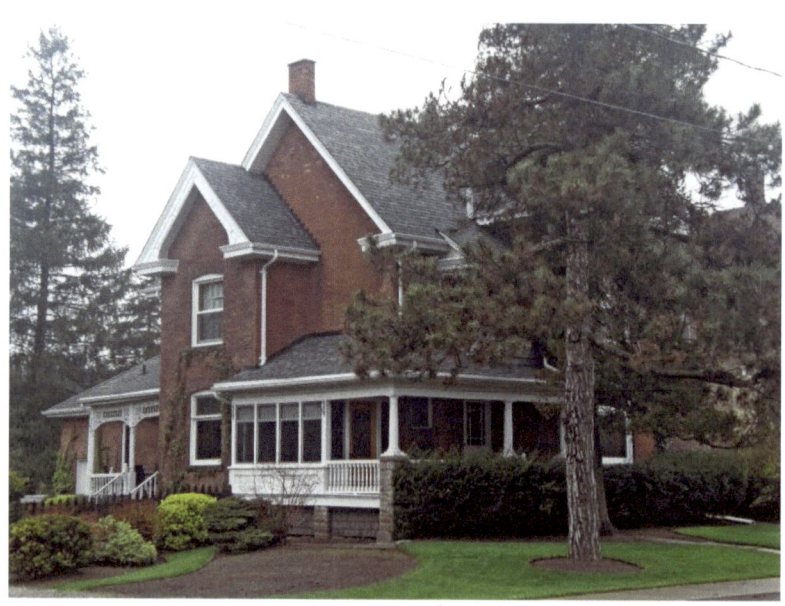

Vernacular

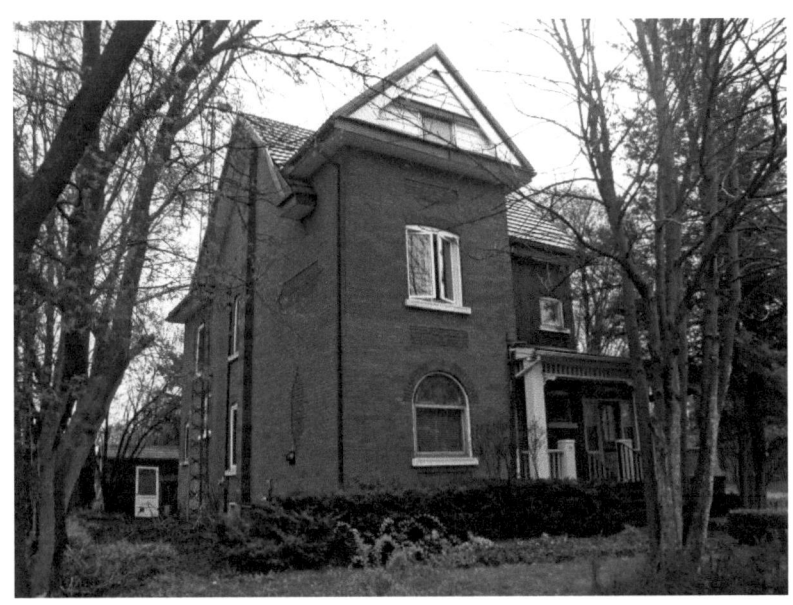

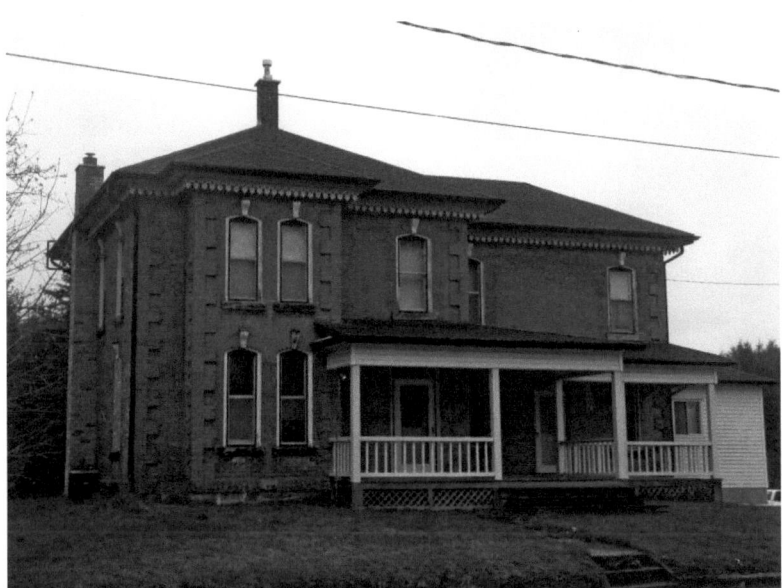

Italianate – hipped roof, decorative cornice, voussoirs with keystones over windows, corner quoins

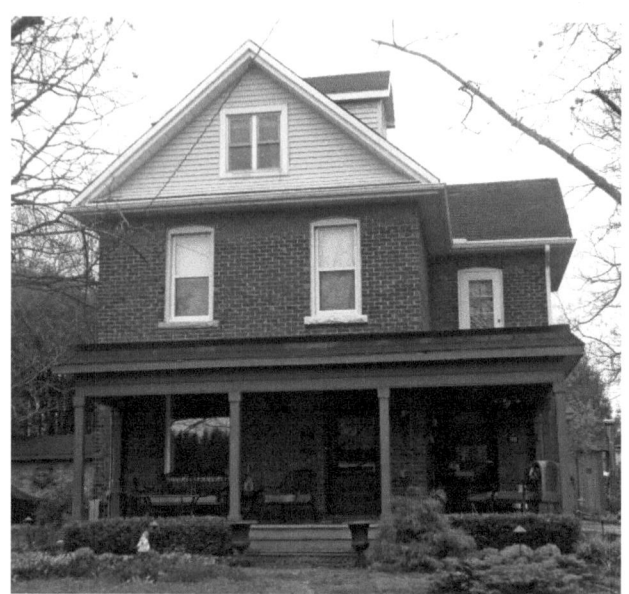

Edwardian - dormer

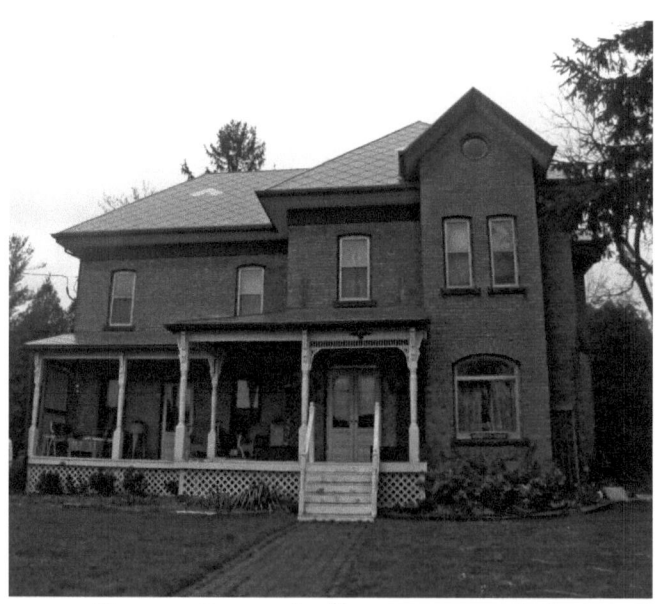

Decorative spindles on verandah

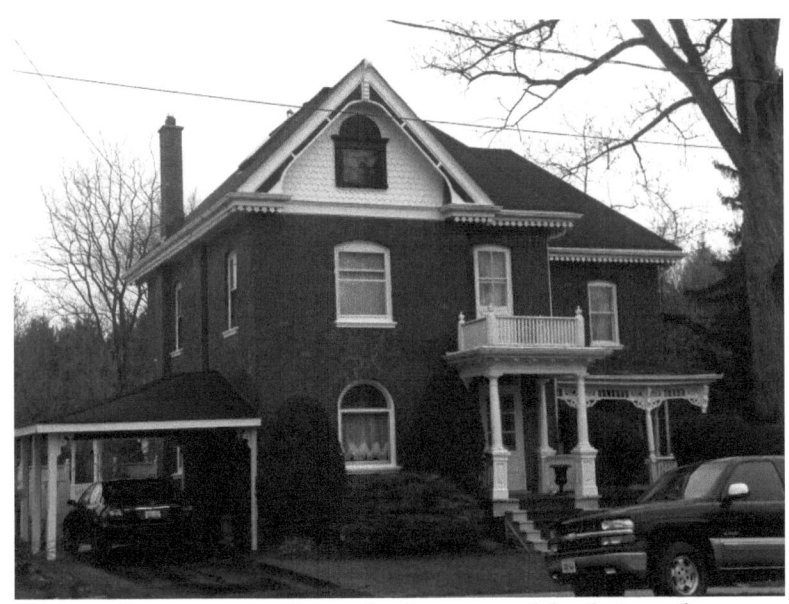

Edwardian – verge board trim on gable, bric-a-brac on verandah, second floor balcony

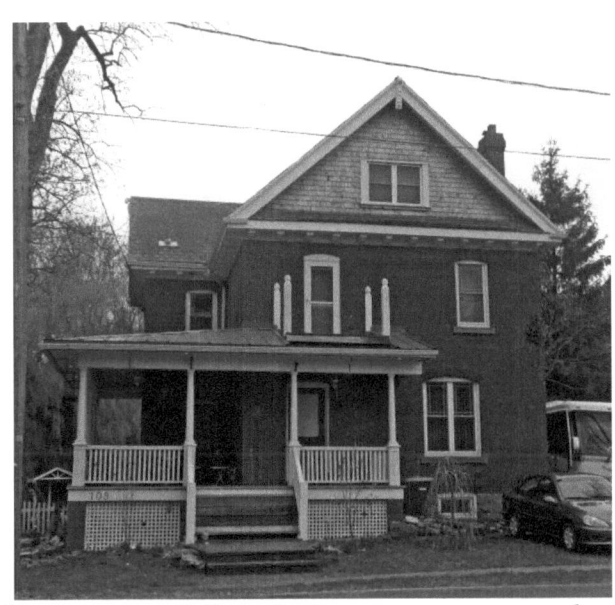

Edwardian – second floor balcony, wraparound verandah

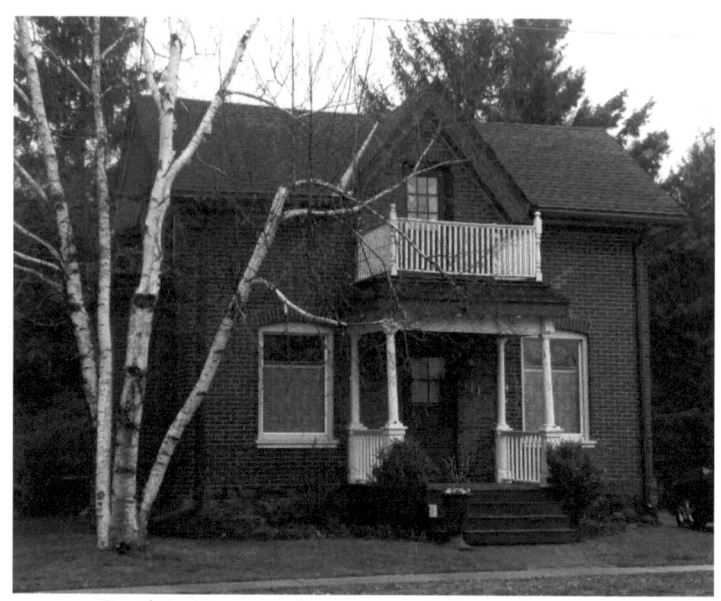

Gothic Revival – second floor balcony

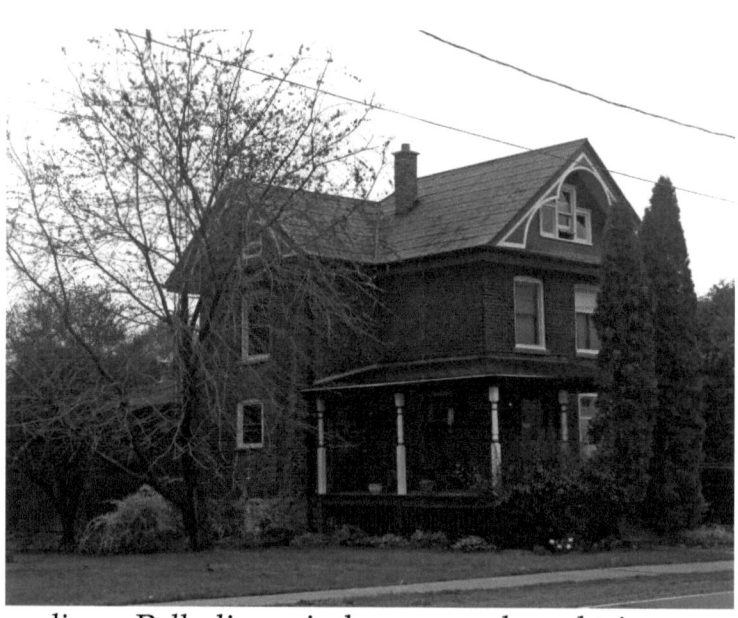

Edwardian – Palladian window, verge board trim on gable,
wood turned spindle verandah supports

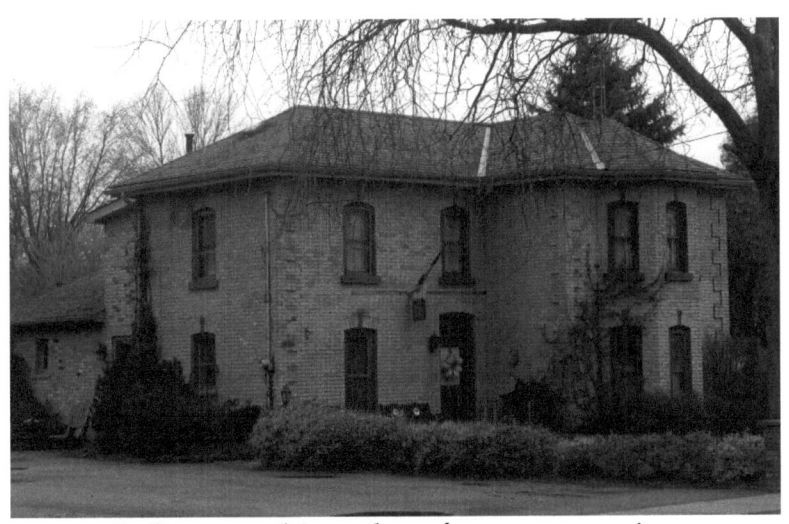

Italianate – hipped roof – corner quoins

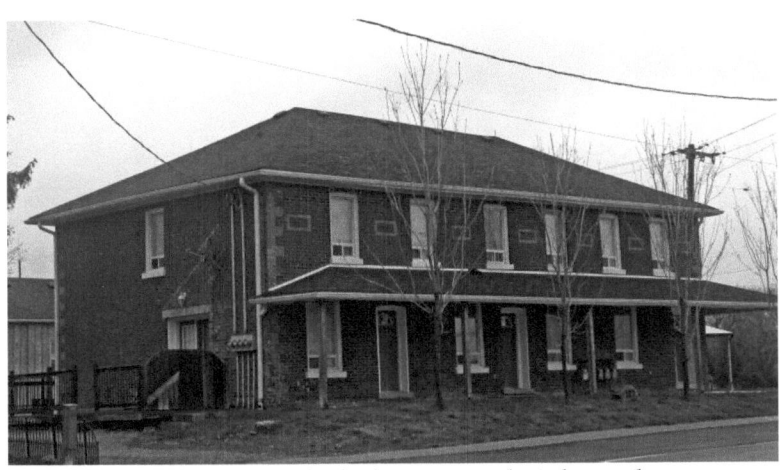

Hipped roof, dichromatic brickwork

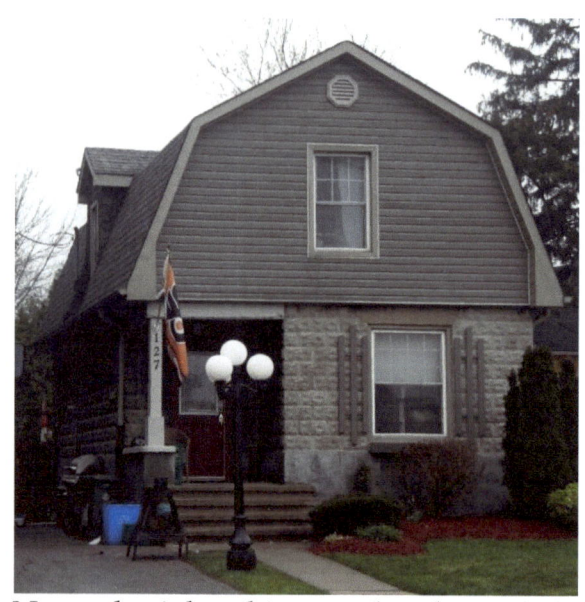

#271 - Neo-colonial architectural style – gambrel roof

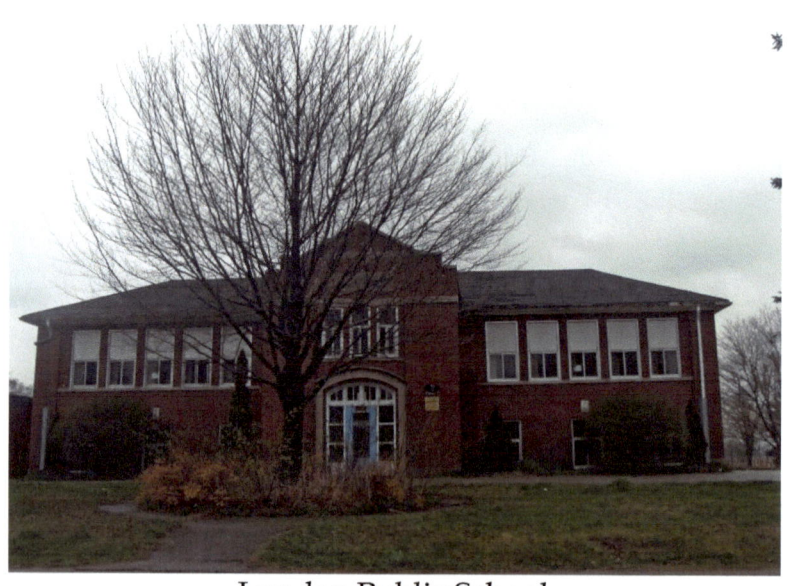

Lynden Public School

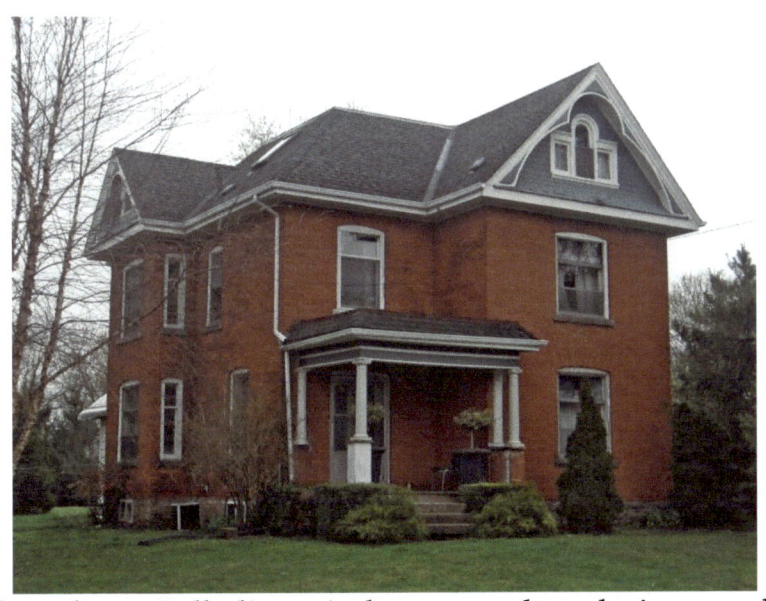

Edwardian – Palladian window, verge board trim on gable

Mount Hope

Gothic Revival - dichromatic brickwork, bay window,
wraparound verandah

Mount Hope is one of the six communities forming The City of Hamilton since its amalgamation in 2001.

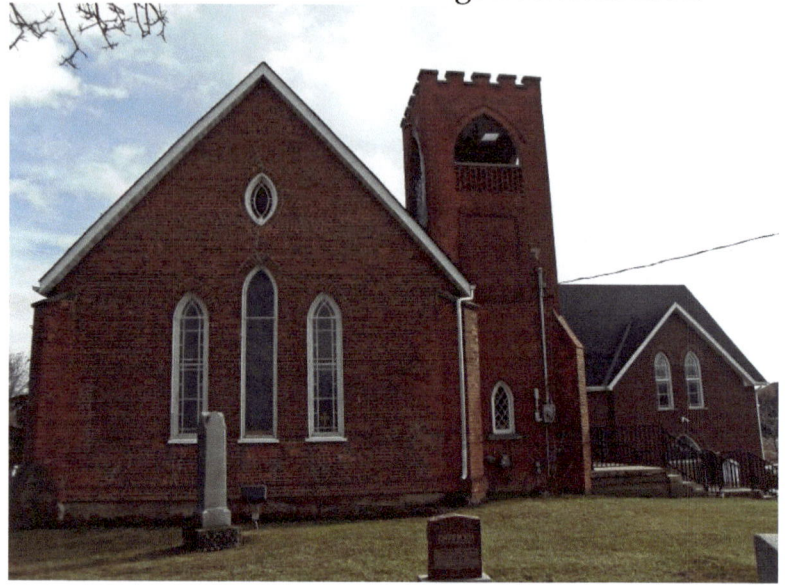

St. Paul's Anglican Church, Glanford – Gothic, lancet windows, buttresses

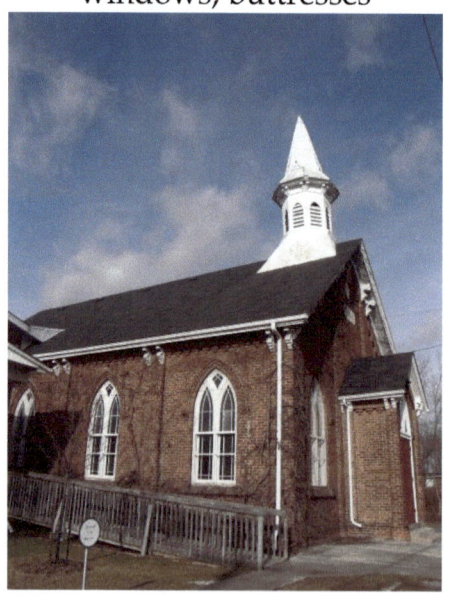

3076 Homestead Drive - Mount Hope United Church, cornice brackets, bevelled dentil moulding, cupola

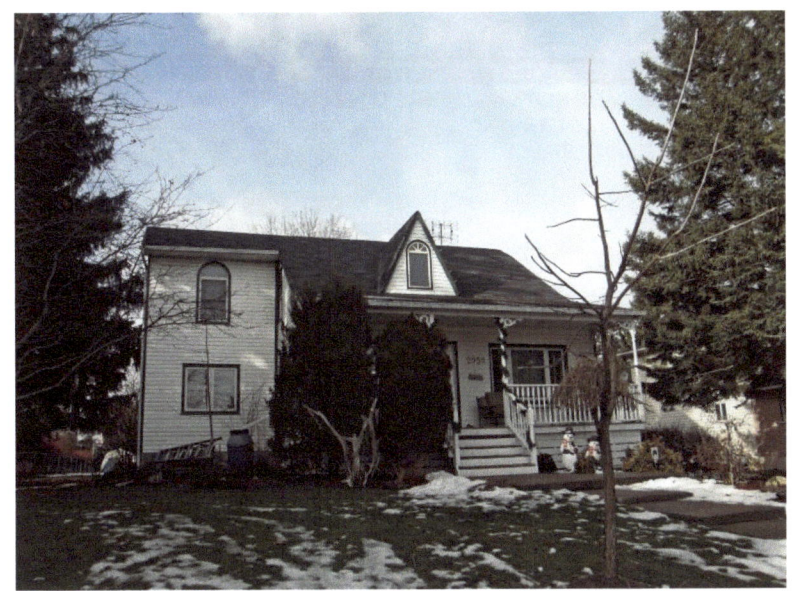

2958 Homestead Drive - Gothic

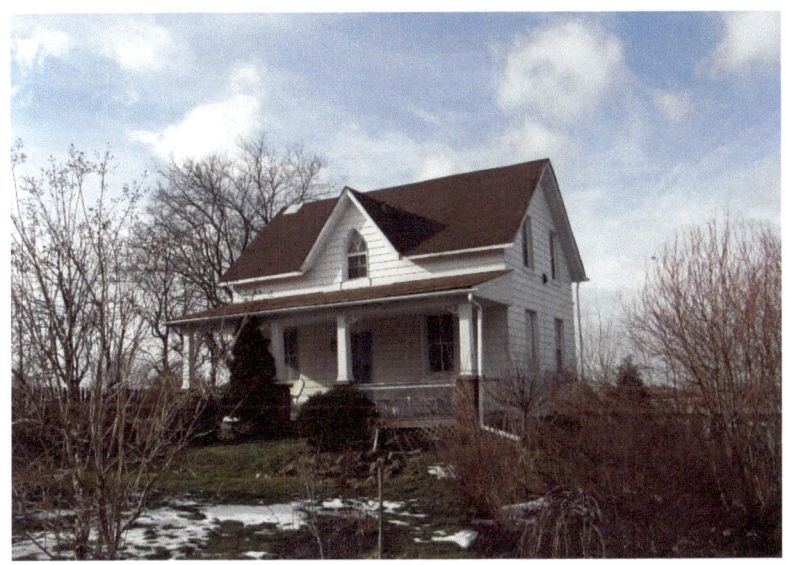

Gothic

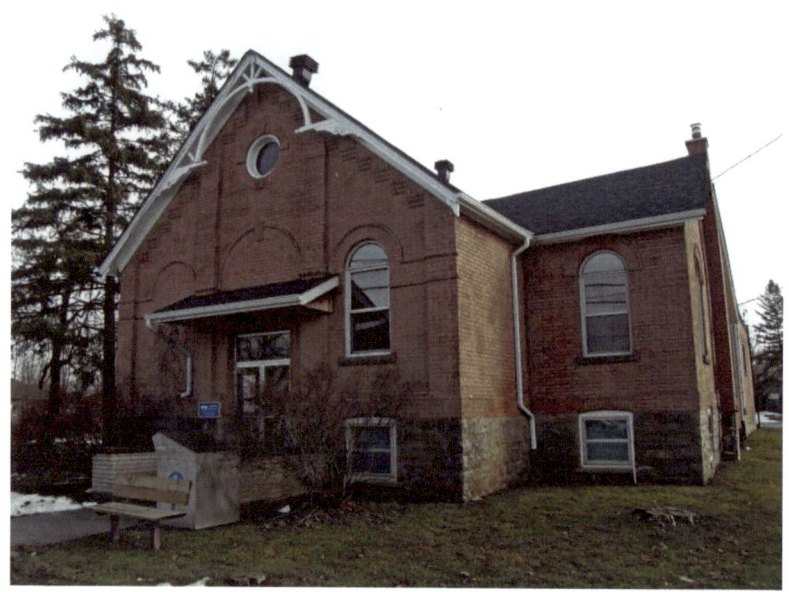

3027 Homestead Drive - In 1990, the former administrative offices of the Township of Glanbrook were renovated for use as Hamilton Public Library Mount Hope. Gothic, verge board trim on gable, voussoirs with keystone above entrance

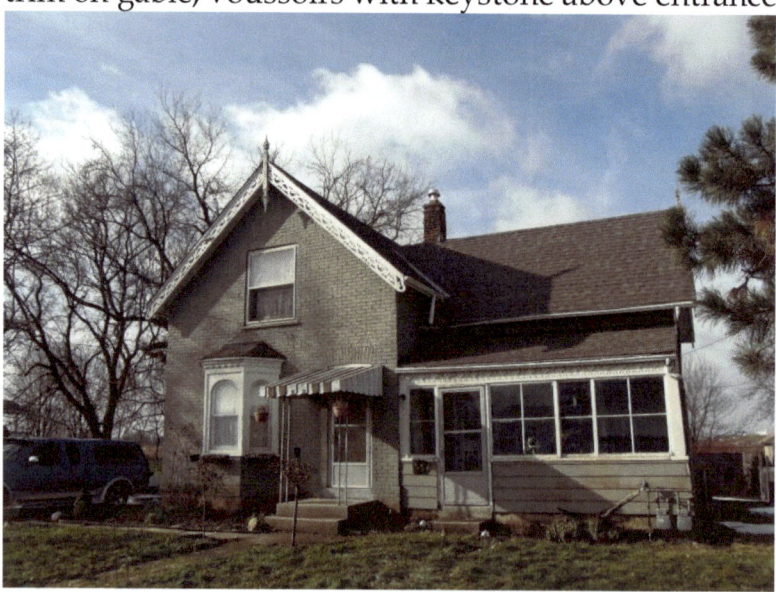

Gothic - verge board and finial on gable

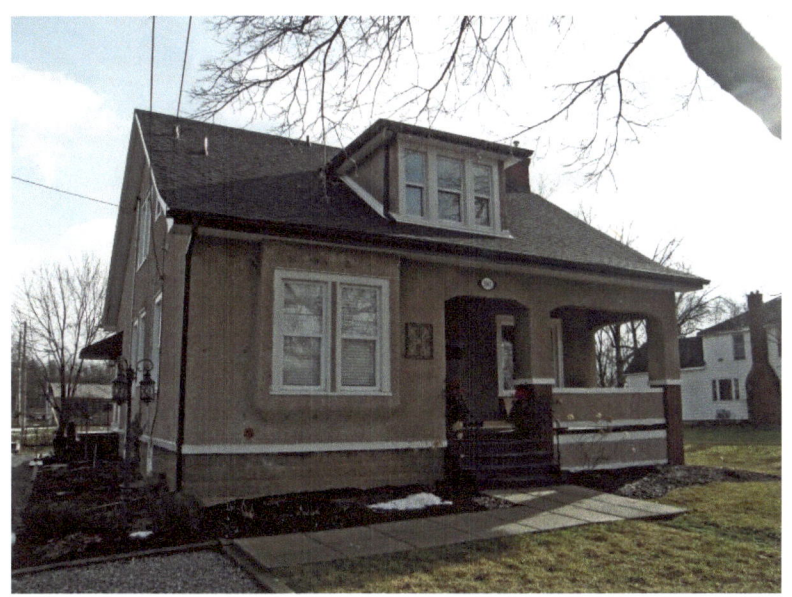

Stucco home #3041 - dormer

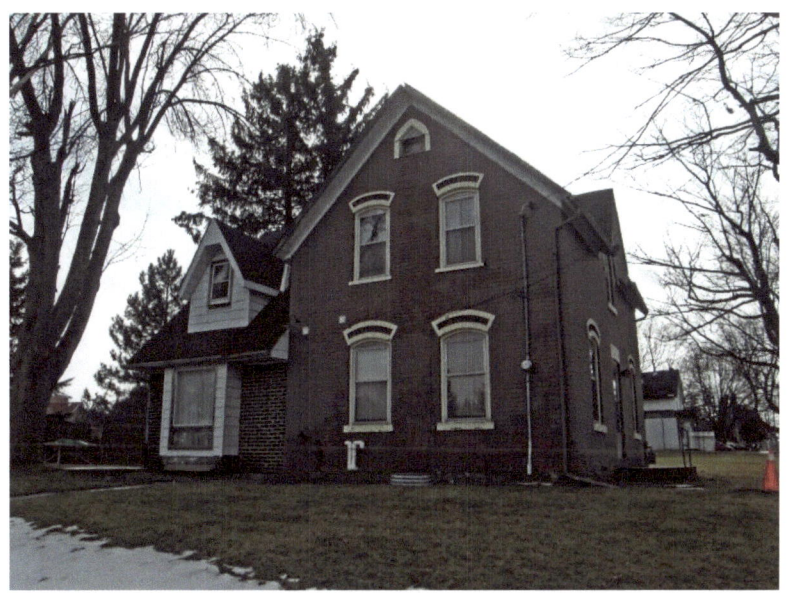

Gothic

John C. Munro Hamilton International Airport, 9300 Airport Road, Mount Hope, was built in October 1940 as a wartime air force training station for flight training, air navigation, telegraphy, and air gunnery. After World War II, the airport became a public facility.

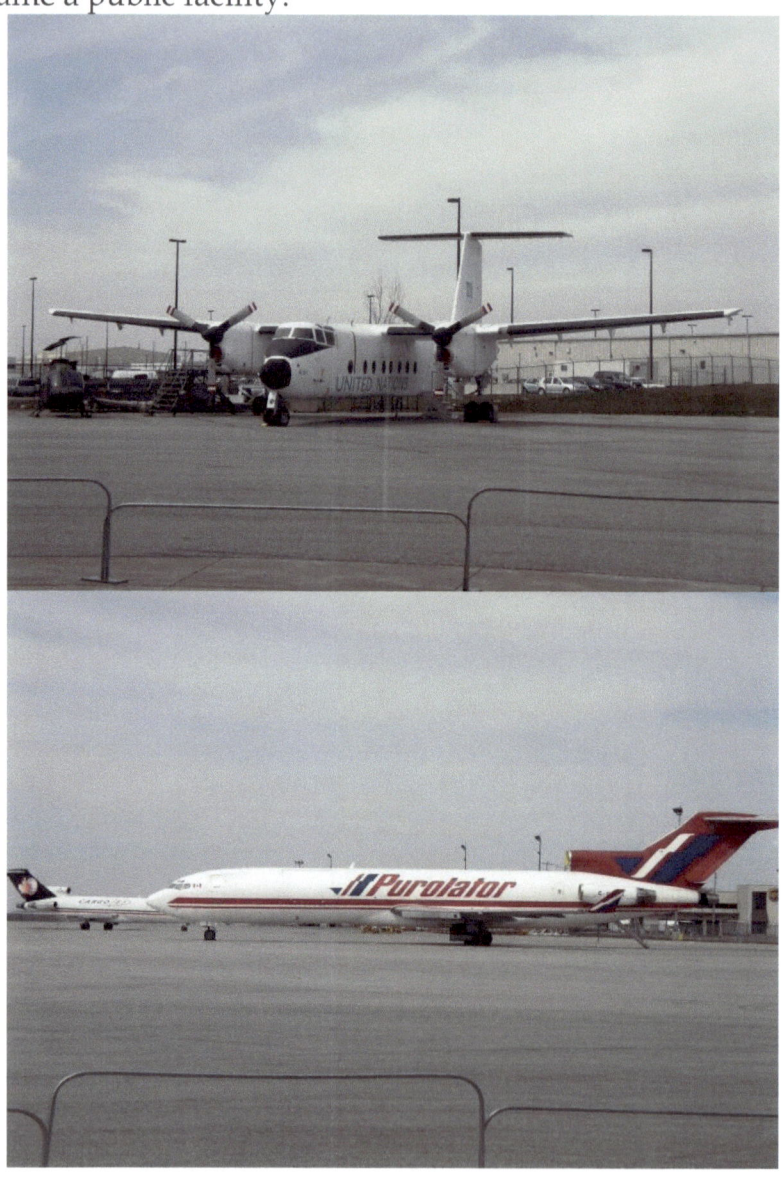

Canadian Warplane Heritage Museum, Mount Hope, with over 25 aircraft in flying condition, features the aircraft used by Canadians and the Canadian Military from the beginning of World War II to the present.

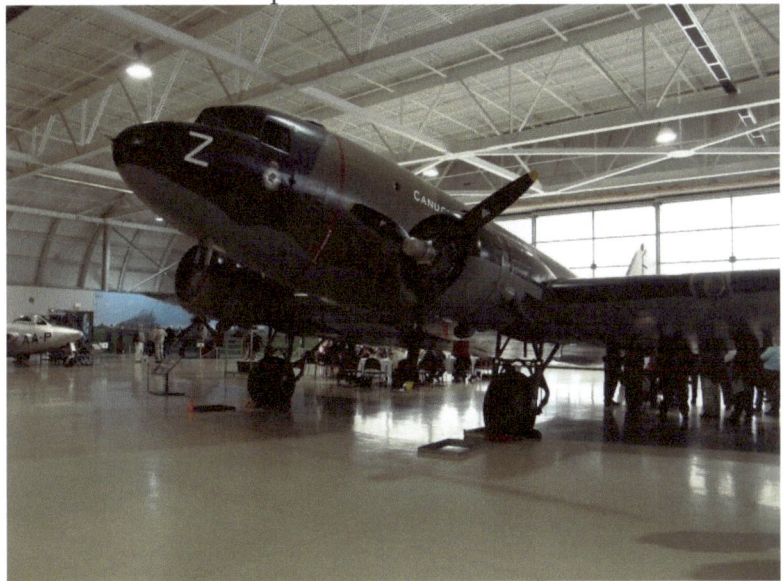

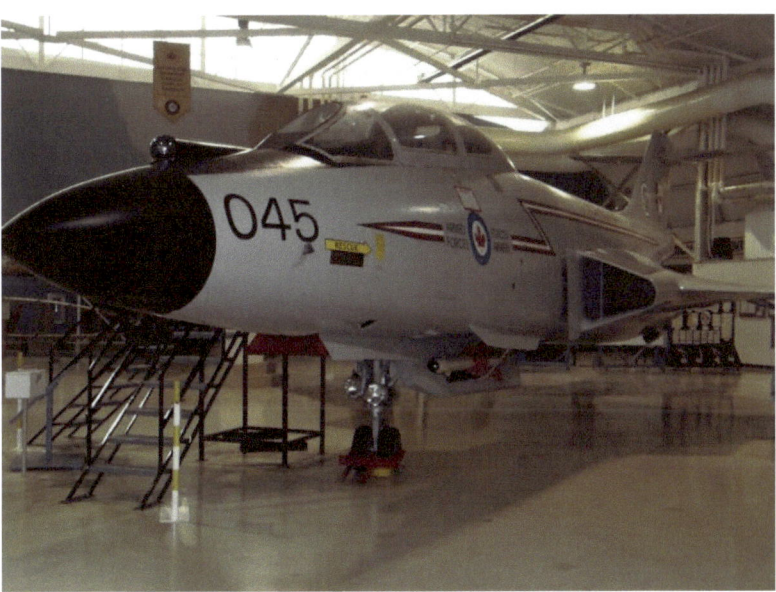

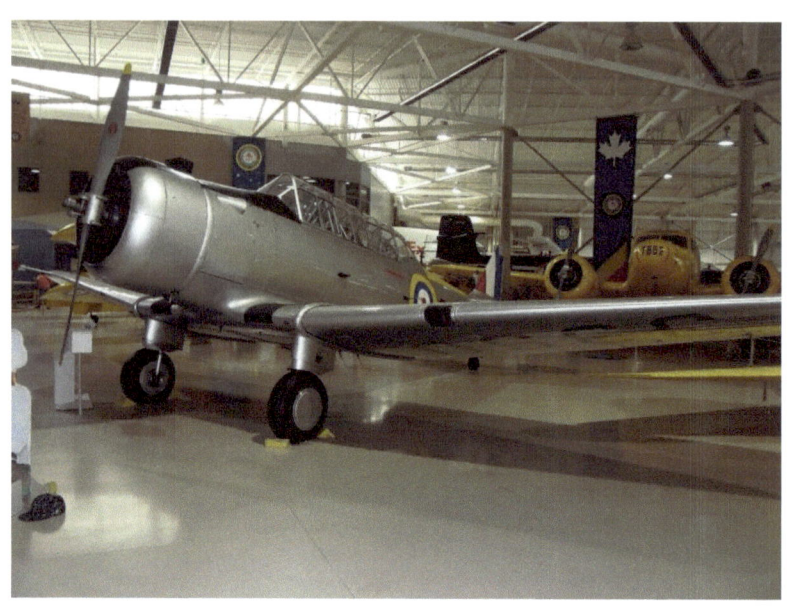

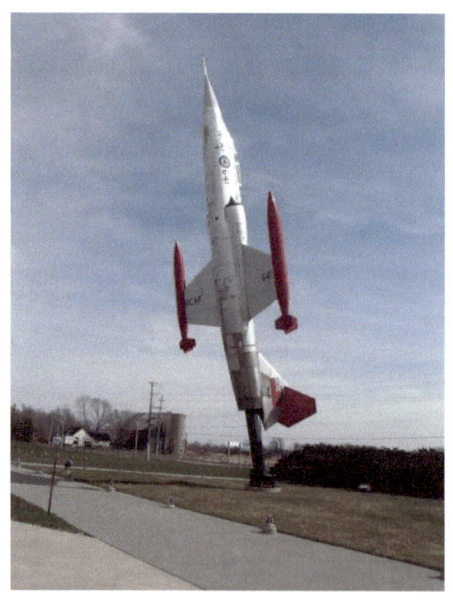

Architectural Terms

Banding: Different materials, colors or textures used in horizontal bands along a wall. Example: Lynden, Page 40	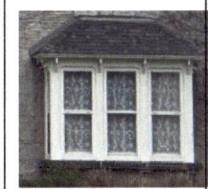
Bay Window: A window that projects out from a wall, in a semicircular, rectangular, or polygonal design. Used frequently in Gothic and Victorian designs. Example: Ancaster, Page 22	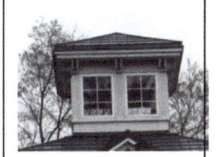
Belvedere: (from the Italian "beautiful view") an architectural feature on a roof, in a garden or on a terrace that gives a beautiful view. Example: 311 Wilson Street East, Ancaster, Page 18	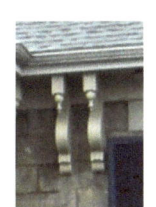
Brackets: a decorative or weight-bearing structural element which forms a right angle with one side against a wall and the other under a projecting surface such as an eave or roof. Example: Ancaster, Page 12	
Buttress: a masonry structure built against or projecting from a wall which serves to support or reinforce the wall. In Canadian architecture, they are sometimes used for decoration. Example: St. Paul's Anglican Church, Glanford, Page 50	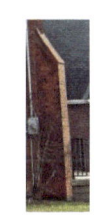

Cobblestone architecture: Refers to the use of cobblestones embedded in mortar as a method for erecting walls on houses and commercial buildings. Example: Ancaster, Page 29	
Cornice: originally the wooden overhang of the roof. With the use of stone, brick, iron and steel, the cornice is any projecting shelf at the top of a ceiling or roof. They can be very decorative. Example: Lynden, Page 39	
Cornice Return: decorative element on the end of a gable. Example: Ancaster, Page 16	
Cupola: A domed or curved roof rising from a building as a decorative element. Example: Ancaster Township Hall, Page 19	
Dichromatic brickwork: the use of two colours of brick, tile or slate to decorate a façade. Example: Mount Hope, Page 49	

Dormer: (French for "sleep") a gable end window that pierces through the plane of a sloping roof surface to create usable space in the top floor or attic of a building by adding headroom. Example: Ancaster Old Mill, Page 10	
Frontispiece: a portion of the façade of a building, usually a centred doorway that is slightly raised from the rest of the building, usually has extensive ornamentation. Frontispieces are usually Classical in design with white columned porches. Example: Ancaster, Page 16	
Gable: the triangular portion of a wall between the edges of a sloping roof. Example: Wilson Street East, Page 14	
Gambrel Roof: a symmetrical two-sided roof with two slopes on each side; the upper slope is positioned at a shallow angle, while the lower slope is steep. It is similar to a mansard roof but a gambrel has vertical gable ends instead of being hipped at the four corners of the building. Example: Lynden, Page 48	
Hipped Roof: a roof where all sides slope downwards to the walls with no gables. Example: Ancaster, Page 16	
Iron Cresting: A decorative ornament along the top of a roof. Iron cresting was popular in the Baroque era and also in Italianate, Victorian, Second Empire and Queen Anne styles of architecture. Example: Lynden, Page 38	

Lancet Window: a tall, narrow window with a pointed arch at its top. Example: St. Paul's Anglican Church, Glanford, Page 35	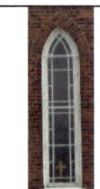
Palladian Window: a large window that is divided into three sections with the centre section larger than the two side sections and usually arched. Example: Lynden, Page 39	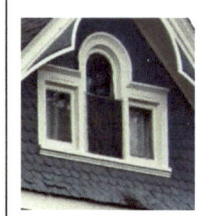
Quoin: masonry blocks at the corner of a wall, often a decorative feature, usually larger or of a different colour than the rest of the wall. Example: 117 Wilson Street West, Ancaster, Page 33	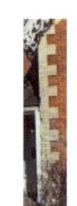
Sidelight: a window, usually with a vertical emphasis, that flanks a door, and is often used to emphasize the importance of a primary entrance. **Transom Window:** the light above the doorway, also called a fanlight. Example: Ancaster, Page 22	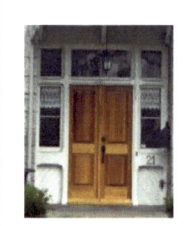
Verge boards: also called bargeboards – hang from the projecting end of a roof and are often elaborately carved and ornamented. Example: 117 Wilson Street West, Ancaster, Page 33	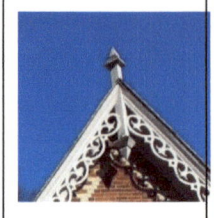

Edwardian, 1900-1930 – This style bridges the ornate and elaborate styles of the Victorian era and the simplified styles of the 20th century. Balanced facades, simple roof lines, dormer windows, large front porches, and smooth brick surfaces are its characteristics. Example: Lynden, Page 39	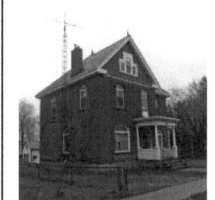
Georgian, before 1860 – This style began with the British King Georges in the 18th century. These buildings have balanced facades around a central door, medium-pitched gable roofs, and small paned windows. Example: Ancaster, Page 27	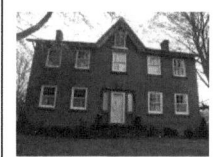
Gothic Revival, 1830-1890 – These decorative buildings have sharply-pitched gables with highly detailed verge boards, pointed-arch window openings, and dichromatic brickwork. It is a common style in Ontario. Example: Ancaster, Page 28	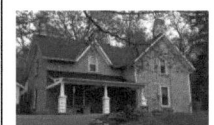

Italianate, 1850-1900 – It has wide-bracketed eaves, belvederes, wrap-around verandahs. Example: Ancaster, Page 22	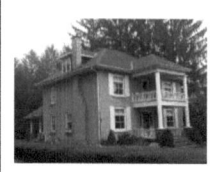
Neo-colonial (also Colonial Revival, Georgian Revival or Neo-Georgian) architecture seeks to revive elements of architectural style of American colonial architecture of the period around the Revolutionary War which drew strongly from Georgian architecture of Great Britain. Architecture from the 18th and early 19th centuries in Ontario includes a wide assortment of detailing and ornament applied to a design centered around the fireplace and the source of water. Structures are typically two stories, have a symmetrical front facade with elaborate front doorways, often with decorative crown pediments, fanlights, and sidelights, symmetrical windows flanking the front entrance, often in pairs or threes, and columned porches. Example: Lynden, Page 48	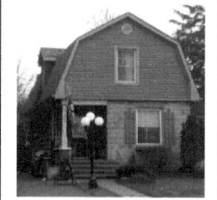
Vernacular/Traditional Mode 1638 - 1950 Influenced but not defined by a particular style, vernacular buildings are made from easily available materials and exhibit local design characteristics. Example: Page 42	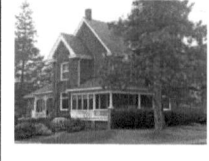